French Revolution

The History and Legacy of the Seminal Events That Began the Uprising in France

(From the Beginning to an End of Revolution History)

Karl Anderson

Published By **Regina Loviusher**

Karl Anderson

All Rights Reserved

French Revolution: The History and Legacy of the Seminal Events That Began the Uprising in France (From the Beginning to an End of Revolution History)

ISBN 978-1-77485-938-4

No part of this guidebook shall be reproduced in any form without permission in writing from the publisher except in the case of brief quotations embodied in critical articles or reviews.

Legal & Disclaimer

The information contained in this ebook is not designed to replace or take the place of any form of medicine or professional medical advice. The information in this ebook has been provided for educational & entertainment purposes only.

The information contained in this book has been compiled from sources deemed reliable, and it is accurate to the best of the Author's knowledge; however, the Author cannot guarantee its accuracy and validity and cannot be held liable for any errors or omissions. Changes are periodically made to this book. You must consult your doctor or get professional medical advice before using any of the suggested remedies, techniques, or information in this book.

Upon using the information contained in this book, you agree to hold harmless the Author from and against any damages, costs, and expenses, including any legal fees potentially resulting from the application of any of the information provided by this guide. This disclaimer applies to any damages or injury caused by the use and application, whether directly or indirectly, of any advice or information presented, whether for breach of contract, tort, negligence, personal injury, criminal intent, or under any other cause of action.

You agree to accept all risks of using the information presented inside this book. You need to consult a professional medical practitioner in order to ensure you are both able and healthy enough to participate in this program.

Table of contents

Chapter 1: What Was The Reign Of Terror All About? 1

Chapter 2: The Absolute Monarchy 10

Chapter 3: First Republic Is Formed 27

Chapter 4: Revolutionary Wars 45

Chapter 5: The Repercussions Of The Revolution 53

Chapter 6: The Gathering Storm 66

Chapter 7: The Background And The French Revolution 119

Chapter 8: Declaration Of The Rights Of Man And Of The Citizen 144

Chapter 1: What was the Reign of Terror All About?

The Reign of terror was a period of significant social and political change in France that began in 1789, when the estates general were established. Estates General and ended in the November 1799 month with the establishment of the French Consulate. A lot of its theories are considered to be important elements of liberal democracy. Likewise, phrases like Liberte as well as egalite and fraternite came back into the scene in subsequent rebellions, including during the Russian Revolution, and stimulated attempts to eradicate the oppression and gain universal vote.

The French government's values and its organizations continue to influence French current politics.

The reasons are generally believed to be a combination of political, social and financial problems which the present system could not resolve.

The Estates-General gathered in 1789 as a response to widespread social discontent and by the month of June they were transformed into an National Assembly. The Assembly approved a variety of significant reforms, including the elimination of feudalism the control of the government over the Catholic Church and the expansion of voting rights.

The fight for political power took over the following three years, heightened by the financial crisis and social unrest. External powers such as Austria, Britain, and Prussia considered that the Revolution as a danger which is why they feared for their own safety. French Revolutionary Wars broke out in April 1792. Louis XVI's demoralization led to the establishment of the First French Republic on September 22nd, 1792. He also saw his execution in January 1793. In June, a revolt in Paris led to that the Committee of Public Security, which was headed by Maximilien Robertspierre replace the Girondins who had ruled in the National Assembly.

This triggered the Reign of Fear, a project to get rid of presumed "counter-revolutionaries" that lasted till July 1794, with over 16,600 people killed in Paris and the provinces. The Republic was faced with a succession of internecine Royalist and Jacobin rebellions, as well as outside rivals; to deal with this it was The French Directory site was able to take control in November 1795. In spite of numerous victories by the army, the war resulted in financial stagnation and political tensions; the Directory site was later changed through the Consulate during November 1799 which was when the Revolutionary period ended.

What was The Revolutionary War Caused by?

The inability of the Ancien Regime to address financial and social inequality is generally regarded as the main cause for the Reign of Terror. Depression, unemployment and high food prices resulted from the rapid growth of population and the failure of the federal government to efficiently fund its debt. This led to a crisis which Louis XVI was not able to manage because of a tax system that was regressive and the ruling class's reluctance to change.

In the same way that it was not restricted to a small elite the discussion of these issues and political discord had migrated into the broader European society. It was believed that certain forms of it of the English "coffeehouse" culture and was spread to other colonized European regions, particularly British Canadians, British US in addition to Canada. Interactions among different communities that were located in Edinburgh, Geneva, Boston, Amsterdam, Paris, London and Vienna were more significant than what most people are aware of.

The concept of elites from around the world sharing ideas and trends was not novel; however, what was different was the extent and the number of people who took part.

The Court of Versailles was the central point of style, culture and political power under Louis XIV. Through the period of 18th-century, advancements in literacy and education resulted in a broader audience for journals and papers including Masonic lodges and coffee houses and reading clubs providing spaces for people to debate and debate ideas. In the wake of the development of the "public sphere" Paris displaced Versailles as the capital of intellectual and cultural life and left the Court in a bind and unable to change the opinion of a well-known view.

Alongside these social changes, French population grew between 18 million people in 1770 to 26 million by 1789. making it the most populous country. Paris was home to more than 600,000 inhabitants, a third of them were unemployed or did not have a regular job.

Domestic farmers faced a difficult time growing enough food for the population due to of their ineffective farming methods as well as outdated transportation networks that caused it to be difficult to distribute even when there was enough. Between 1770 and 1790, food prices increased by 65 percent while wages just grew to 22 percent. The dictatorship was plagued by such shortages in part because many blamed the cost of living to the government's inability to put a stop to the profiteering. A disappointing harvest that was followed by a severe winter resulted in a rural population without a single commodity to sell and a city-based proletariat that had only a few dollars to spend by the spring of 1789.

The state financial obligation was the second significant economic burden. Traditional reports for the Reign of terror regularly blame the financial crisis on the cost from the Anglo-French War of 1778 to 1783. However, more recent analysis of the financial market reveal that this is just a small part of the picture. In 1788 France was in debt to GDP ratios at 55.6 percent, which was lower than 181.8 percentage in UK however, while the expenses were greater in France but the percentage of money that was devoted for interest payment was nearly identical across both countries. "Neither the size in French government debts in 1788, or its prior historical context, can be considered as a proof of the onset of revolution that took place in 1789" According to one scholar.

The issue was brought about by the taxing system which was employed to fund the federal government's spending. Although it is generally believed that the clergy and nobles were generally exempt from taxation but more recent studies suggest that the burden of tax was more evenly distributed between the classes than was previously was believed, yet the method of assessing and collecting it was "a disaster." Tax rates vary greatly between regions, typically had no relationship to major decrees and were collected in a variety of ways and it was that "overwelming complex system" which sparked hatred just as much as the tax rate itself. Local Parlements who governed the policy of monetary, were opposed to attempts to simplify the system. The resultant impasse in the face of widespread financial hardship, prompted the Estates General to gather that was later radicalized by the battle to control public resources.

Despite being at all apathetic to the issue and even aspiring to think about changes, Louis XVI often pulled back when confronted by conservative Aristocrats.

The court, specifically Queen Marie-Antoinette whom was seen as a shady Austrian spy, and accused of removing ministers who were 'progressive' such as Jacques Necker, ended up being the subject of a lot of anger. Ideas of the equality of people and democracy gave an intellectual framework for dealing with these challenges for those who challenged it and it was the American Revolution was viewed as an acknowledgement of their value.

Chapter 2: The Absolute Monarchy

The modest reforms proved to be too to Marie Antoinette and Louis' younger brother who was the Comte d'Artois. The latter suggested to Louis to replace Necker as his primary minister on the 11th of July. Following reports that Necker planned to use his Swiss Guards to oblige the Assembly to end its session in a matter of hours, the Assembly began a continuous session on the 12th of July. A large number of protesters took to the streets following the declaration, and warriors of an elite Gardes Francaises system refused to distribute the delegates.

Many of them joined the mob for an assault on the Bastille the magnificent stronghold that was stocked with ammunition and weapons, on July 14. After a few hours of fighting and announcing the deaths of 83 attackers and the ruler de Launay gave up. He was detained at the Hotel de Ville, where the execution took place and he paraded around the city with his head resting on pikes. The castle was destroyed within an extremely short period of. The Bastille contained only seven hostages despite reports that claimed otherwise including 4 forgers, 2 nobles arrested for "unethical behavior," and a murder suspect. As a image that embodied an Ancien Regime, its fall was celebrated as a triumph as well Bastille Day is still honored every year.

In a bid to regain control of Paris, Louis designated Lafayette as the leader for his National Guard and Jean-Sylvain Bailly as the president of the Commune which was a new administration body. On the 17th of July when he arrived to Paris along with 100 lawmakers which was received by Bailly and presented with a tricolore-cockade to a roaring applause. It was clear that the authority had departed out of his palace. He was honored as 'LouisXVI father of the French and queen of an entirely independent nation.'

The temporary unity of the Assembly, imposed by a single threat quickly dissolved. Deputies quarreled about constitutional rules Civil power deteriorated swiftly. A Parisian mob killed Finance Minister Joseph Foullon and his child on the 22nd of July and neither Bailly or Lafayette could stop the violence. Fear and rumors of violence of the countryside led to the use of militias and the agrarian rebellion known as the Grande Peur. The breakdown in law and order, as well as the frequent attacks on property that were fashionable, led a significant portion of nobility entrust other nations. Those emigres backed counter-revolutionary groups in France and lobbied foreign emperors to support them.

In response to this, the Assembly came up with the August Decrees that ended feudalism as well as other upper-class opportunities, not only tax exemption. Other decrees included equality in the face of the law, accessibility of all public places of employment religious liberty, as well as the elimination of specific opportunities offered by towns and provinces. More than 25% of French agricultural land was subject to feudal charges that paid a substantial compensation for landowners who were wealthy as well as the tithes due to the church, are now removed. The idea was to allow renters to cover their loss, but the majority were against it, and the plan was changed in 1793.

The suspension of thirteen local parlements during November was the conclusion of the prior program's main institution-building pillars in just four months. The Revolution also revealed hints of its radical nature from beginning; however, what remained unclear was the constitution's structure to translate ideas into practical applications.

With the assistance from Thomas Jefferson, Lafayette prepared with the help of Thomas Jefferson, Lafayette drafted the Statement of the Rights of Man and Person which was which was a constitution proposal that reiterated certain of the provisions of the Declaration. However there was no agreement in France regarding the role of the Crown and it was not feasible to create political groups until this issue was addressed. When the document was put before members of the committee for legal on the 11th of July the pragmatists, like the Jean Joseph Mounier, the President of the Assembly Jean Joseph Mounier, who emphasized the need for developing unrealistic expectations, rejected the idea.

It was published on August 26th, as a declaration of idea after it was modified by Mirabeau.

The language contained elements that could have been deemed as a serious issue within any European society and 1789 was not the least of them. France and, while historians and experts debate who is responsible for the language of the time, many think that there is a mixture. Despite the fact that Jefferson was a major contributor to Lafayette's draft, he also acknowledged the intellectual responsibility of Montesquieu and the final formulation differed greatly. The document "highlighted egalitarianism in a manner which (the) American Declaration did not. (American Declaration) did not," according to French historian Georges Lefebvre and was accompanied by the removal of the advantage and feudalism.

In addition the two groups' intentions diverged. Jefferson was of the opinion that his views on the USA Constitution and Bill of Rights as a way to establish the system of government in a particular moment and claimed that they "included no thought ... however, they were a representation of what was known as the American mind" in the moment.

The Statement gave an aspirational view, which is the primary distinction between the two transformations. In the first, the French Constitution of 1791 was considered to be a point of departure and the Statement providing an aspirational goal. It was included in the current French Constitution in the year 1958, as a beginning point to that of the French Constitution of 1791 and the one in that of the French Third Republic from 1870 up to 1940.

The squabbles continued. Mounier, who was backed by conservatives, such as Gerard de Lally-Tollendal, pushed the idea of an bicameral, federal government that included an upper house that was ruled by a king with the right to veto. On September 10, a majority headed by Sieyes and Talleyrand rejected this idea to create an assembly of one which left Louis with only the power of a "suspensive veto" which allowed the president to delay but not block the implementation of legislation. An entirely new commission was created from this base to create the constitution. The most controversial topic was citizenship, which was linked to the dispute regarding the proportionality of individual rights and obligations. The 1791 Constitution established a distinction between "active residents" with the right to vote, which was described as French males above 25 years old that paid taxes direct equal to three days' work as well as 'passive citizens with only 'civil rights.' This is why it was never fully recognized by Jacobin club's extremes.

Food shortages and a degrading economy caused a lot of people to be unhappy with the lack of development in addition, people of the Parisian middle class also known as"the "sans culottes" ended up being a bit discontented. The worst of it was in the latter part of September in the late September when people from the Flanders Program showed up in Versailles to strengthen the Royal Bodyguard, and was presented with a lavish meal according to tradition. Reports of the event in the press described it were described as an "gluttonous orgie" and claims of the tricolor-cockade was been mistreated, sparked public outrage. The soldiers' appearance was also considered to be an attempt to intimidate the Assembly.

Women gathered in large numbers at the Hotel de Ville on October 5th, 1789to demand the hotel to lower its rates and improve bread supply.

These protests quickly became political and, following the acquisition of guns from Hotel de Ville, 7,000 participants took to Versailles where they addressed their concerns in the Assembly. They were rebuffed by about 15,000 Guardsmen of the National Guard commanded by Lafayette who at first attempted to deter them, but eventually resorted to taking over management when it became clear that they'd be leaving when he failed to meet their demands.

In the evening, when it was the time that National Guard came, Lafayette was able to convince Louis to move the family of his to Paris was essential to ensure their safety. A group of protesters broke into the royal quarters early morning, looking for Marie Antoinette, who had quit. They sacked the palace, and killed several guards as they did so. In spite of the difficulty it was finally restored as was the

Royal family as well as the Assembly were taken by Paris with guards from the National Guard. Louis declared his support for absolute monarchy, revealing his acceptance of the August Decrees and Declaration, and his officially recognized title was changed from "King Of France and 'King of the French.'

According to historian John McManners, "throne and altar were frequently portrayed as being closely linked in the 18th century France and their simultaneous collapse ... will eventually provide the conclusive evidence of their relationship." One theory is that following a long period of oppression and persecution, a few French Protestants were actively promoting an anti-Catholic dictatorshipthat was fueled by Knowledge thinkers such as Voltaire. It was "manifestly against the laws in nature ... it was a pity that some people consume themselves in excess as the rest of the population goes without need," wrote thinker Jean-Jacques Rousseau.

While the legitimacy of religious practice has been questioned however, the Revolution resulted in a significant shift in authority away from that of the Catholic church to state. The reduction in tolerance of spiritual minorities led to the fact that by 1789 the term "being" French also was a sign of being Catholic.

In France, the church was also its most powerful individual landowner, with around 10% of the estates as well as gathering tithes which was a successful 10% income tax, on salaries and peasant farmers as a form of crop. In exchange, it offered very little social assistance.

The Assembly removed tithes in the month of August. Then, in November 2, it confiscated all property belonging to the church that was worth its value. was used to finance the assignats, a brand new paper currency. The government agreed to take on obligations such as paying clergy and providing for the poor, sick and orphaned. Abbeys and spiritual societies were closed on the 13th of February 1790. Monks and nuns were encouraged to return to civilian lives.

A Clergy's Civil Constitution of July the 12th 1790 created them as state employees, established wages, and created the method of choosing bishops and priests. Many French Catholics, which includes Pope Pius VI, opposed to this because it weakened the power of Pope Francis on and control over French Church. Thirty bishops signed a document that slammed the law in October, which contributed to the demonstration.

In some instances, historians view that the Legal Assembly as ineffective, in a discussion of the role of the monarchy. These have been exacerbated due to Louis his reluctance to impose restrictions on his power, and his efforts to end them with external assistance. Just four of the six million Frenchmen who were over 25 were able to vote, as the franchise was restricted to those who paid a minimal amount of taxes and largely excluded the without culottes, or the city's working class, who largely felt that the new government was not meeting their demands for food and employment.

In the end, large factions, both within and outside of the Assembly that was divided into three main groups, were against the constitution that was adopted. 245 members were Barnave's Feuillants constitutional monarchists who believed that the Revolution was too far. Another 13 were Jacobin leftists who wanted the establishment of a republic under Brissot and often referred to as Brissotins. The remaining 345 were part of La Plaine, a centrist faction that changed votes based on the subject and many agreed with Brissotin's reservations regarding Louis his commitment towards the Revolution. "Vive le return of investment, s'il est de bonne foi!" Or "Long live the King - insofar as he stays true to promises!" was a comment made after Louis was officially signed his new Constitution.

Although they were an outlier however, the Brissotins have control over vital committees allowed them to concentrate on two subjects that were developed to demonstrate Louis as anti-Revolutionary , by urging Louis to exercise his veto. The first one was about emigrants. the Assembly passed legislation that took their possessions as well as threatened with a death penalty between the months of October until November. The second group of non-juring priestswhose opposition towards Constitutional law Civil Constitution led to a state of war that was almost civil in the southern part of France and southern France, which Bernave attempted to ease by relaxing the stricter restrictions. The Assembly adopted an order on the 29th of November and gave the clergy in rebellion eight days to comply or face accusations of conspiracy against the country that even Robespierre believed was a step too far and too quickly. Both were barred by Louis who was not surprised.

It was followed by a war program that targeted Austria and Prussia that was initiated from Brissot and whose goals are described as a blend of negative assessment and innovative ideaslism. The project expressed a fervent belief in the propagation of political freedom and well-known sovereignty and leveraging the well-known anti-Austrian beliefs. In a paradox, Marie Antoinette led a court group that favored the war as a means to regain control of the army and restore the noble power. Louis spoke at the Assembly during November 1791. offering foreign powers the option of distributing the refugees or risk war. The issue was discussed with passion by those who supported it and skepticism by the challengers.

Bernave's inability to agree to an agreement in the Assembly resulted in the formation of a new administration comprised of Brissotins. In 1792, the French Revolutionary Wars started on the 20th of April 1792 as France's army attacked Austrian as well as Prussian forces on their border and suffered humiliating beatings. The federal government required non-juring priests swear the oath, or else risk being deported as well as liquified the Constitutional Guard and changed it by adding 20,000 federes as an effort to gain popular support. Louis accepted the decision to dissolving the Guard however, he resisted two other propositions and Lafayette approached the Assembly to cut down on the clubs.

The first day of August, the news of the Brunswick Manifesto reached Paris, warning of 'memorable retribution' if anyone opposed to the Allies efforts to restore monarchy rule. It was reported that the Tuileries Palace was attacked by the combined forces from the Parisian National Guard and provincial federes in the morning of the 10th of August which killed a lot of Swiss Guardsmen who were guarding the palace. Louis along with his wife scoured for sanctuary through the Assembly that voted shortly at around

11:00 a.m. to temporarily remove the king, thereby disbanding the monarchy.

Chapter 3: First Republic Is Formed

The elections of the National Convention were place in the latter part of August. The restrictions on citizens have reduced the number of ballots that were cast down up to 3.3 million, a fraction of the four million in 1791. Additionally, intimidation was common. The former Brissotins have been divided into two groups which are the moderate Girondins who are headed by Brissot and the ferocious Montagnards led by Maximilien Robespierre Georges Danton, and Jean-Paul Marat. About 160 of the 749 deputy deputies were Girondists, 200 Montagnards and 389 were members from La Plaine, regardless of shifting loyalties. The center-right faction, led by Bertrand Barere, Pierre Joseph Cambon as well as Lazare Carnot, voted as a swing vote just like before.

Between 1,100 and 1,600 prisoners who were seized within Parisian prisons were executed in the aftermath of the

September Massacres and the majority of them were minor criminals. The perpetrators were mostly Country Guard men and federes who were headed to the front line in response to the Prussian capture of Longwy along with Verdun. The deaths revealed a general fear about social chaos and moderates voiced support for the actions that quickly spread to the provinces.

On the 20th of September, French soldiers defeated their Prussians at Valmy in a stunning victory. Infuriated by the victory, the Convention altered the monarchy by establishing it becoming the French First Republic on September 22nd. They also established the new calendar and designated the year 1792 "Year One." Trial of Citoyen Louis Capet, formerly Louis XVI, occupied the subsequent months. Although the Convention was divided over the guilt of his accusers, radicals centered on his Jacobin club and Paris Commune were present. The Brunswick Manifesto was the first step to portray Louis as a revolutionary threat. The picture was amplified when excerpts of his personal correspondence were released and revealed his association with Royalist exiles who were serving as part of Prussian and Austrian forces. Prussian as well as Austrian forces.

The Assembly passed a verdict putting Louis to execution for "conspiracy against liberty for the general public and security in general" 17 January 1793, in a vote of 361 against 288. The remaining 72 members voted to execute the man subject to certain conditions. On the 21st day January, verdict was carried out at the Place de la Revolution, which is now known as"the Place de la Concorde. In February the Convention anticipated this by announcing the declaration of war against both the U.K. and the Dutch Republic and the Netherlands Republic. These countries were eventually joined the help of Spain, Portugal, Naples and Tuscany during the War of the First Union.

The Girondins believed they could bring together all those in the federal government and provide an explanation for the rising prices and food shortages however, they found themselves in conflict with the public at large. A lot of people were transferred to provinces. On February 24 the very first conscription mass exercise known as the levee in masse led to protests in Paris and in other cities. Discontented by the church reforms, the typically conservative royalist Vendee was ablaze at the beginning of March. Dumouriez was defeated by Neerwinden in the early hours of 18th of March and he left for the Austrians. Bordeaux, Lyon, Toulon, Marseilles, and Caen were also the scene of uprisings. The Republic seemed to be on the verge of collapse.

The Committee of Public Security, an executive committee that is accountable for the convention created as a result of the conflict on the sixth of April, 1793. The Girondins committed a grave political error by accusing Marat as the one who ordered the massacres of September prior to that of the Revolutionary Tribunal; he was quickly cleared of the charge, thus creating a divide between them from Girondins from the non-culottes. On May 24 the 24th of May, Jacques Hebert required a well-known revolt against the Louis Capet's "henchmen," he was imprisoned at the Commission of Twelve, a predominantly Girondin-dominated court charged with disclosing "plots." To counter the Commune's protests The Commission warned that "if anything happens to officers of the country as a result of your constant disobedience ... Paris would be destroyed."

The clubs had the capability to take on the Girondins, as their animosity increased. On May 31st, they staged an attempted coup, with the assistance of the Commune and a portion from the National Guard. Regardless of the success to halt the plot, a crowd of up to 80,000 attended the convention on June second, demanding food at low cost pay for jobless, as well as political reforms. This is why they restricted the vote to those who are not culottes, and the ability to rebuke lawmakers on the spur of the moment. The Montagnards have taken over the Committee of Public Security on June 10 and there were 10 commission members as well as an additional 29 people from the Girondin party were detained.

Meanwhile, an committee headed by Saint-Just who was who was a close ally of Robespierre was tasked with drafting an updated Constitution. It was disbanded at the 24th of June in just 8 days of work. It included a number of significant reforms, including universal male suffrage as well as the end of serfdom within French possessions. The murder of Marat on the 13th of July, 1793 in 1793 by Girondist Charlotte Corday, which was used by the Committee of Public Security used as a reason to gain authority, halted the standard legal procedure. In October 1793, it was decided that the 1793 Constitution was rescinded forever.

The federal government's priority was to establish an ideology for the state and control the economy and to win the war. Whereas some areas like Vendee and Brittany were seeking to restoration of the monarchy, the majority agreed with the Republic however they opposed the policy in Paris which was a major factor in the vital task of quelling internal discontent. The Convention allowed a second levee in masse on the 17th of August 17, and even though there were initial problems in preparing and supplying massive soldiers, Republican forces had retaken Lyon, Marseilles, and Bordeaux at the beginning of October, fighting Union forces at Hondschoote as well as Wattignies.

The Reign of Horror started as an opportunity to transport enthusiasm for innovation however, it soon devolved into a method to settle personal rifts. The Convention established cost-limits on a range of goods, and the death penalty for hoarders towards time of its end in July and advanced groups were formed on

September 9 to take them to execution. In 1794, the Law of Suspects was enacted on the 17thof September, and enacted the detention of those who believed in the "nemesis of flexibility" beginning what would end up being referred to as"the "Fear." According to archival sources, 16,600 individuals were executed on accusations of counter-revolutionary participation between September 1793 and July 1794; another 40,000 could have been summarily hanged or passed away while waiting on trial.

The improved rates, the death penalty for "profiteers" or hoarders as well as the confiscation of grain stocks by workers in armour resulted in the fact that, by September, Paris was experiencing serious food shortages. However, managing the massive public financial debt that was accumulated through the old practice, which continued to increase due to the conflict, was the biggest burden. The financial debt was first subventioned by the selling of confiscated property, but this proved not to be effective because only a few were able to acquire properties that could be taken back. Financial stability could only be developed by continuing the war till the French counter-revolutionaries were squashed. The situation got more dire when external and internal problems to the Republic were imposed the Republic with a plethora of problems. Managing this via printing assignments led to an increase in inflation and costs.

The Convention recognized that the Committee of Public Security as the supreme Revolutionary Federal government on October 10th. The Constitution was rescinded until peace could be achieved.

Marie Antoinette was condemned of many crimes and was guillotined mid-October. Two weeks later she was executed. Girondist leaders who were locked up in June, along with Philippe Egalite. They were all executed. The horror was not restricted to Paris After the recovery of Lyons about 2500 people were killed.

On the 17th of October the Republican political army defeated the Vendee rebels at Cholet and the survivors fled to Brittany. Although the rebellion was not over until 1796, a second defeat to Le Mans on December twenty-three ended the rebellion as a quite serious risk. Since the middle of the nineteenth century, French historiographers have questioned the severity of the violence that ensued. More than 4,000 people killed in the Loire during the Battle of Nantes between the months of November 1793 to February 1794 at the direction of Jean-Baptiste Provider. According to historian Reynald Schercher, 117,000 persons died between 1793 until 1796. Francois Furet specified that the data "not only revealed massacre and destruction on an unprecedented size, but also a determination so strong that it's given the region a lot of its heritage as its own."

Even advocates of the Horror were not immune from suspicion at the height of the Horror, since even the tiniest idea of counter-revolutionary thought might result in suspicion. In the midst of adversity that arose, schisms erupted among the Montagnard faction that resulted in violent clashes between the extreme Hebertists as well as Danton's moderates. Robespierre considered their struggle as an attempt to undermine the state and as an atheist, he opposed the atheist's anti-religious policies and led to his detention and execution on March 24, along with 19 colleagues, including Provider. To ensure that the making the Hebertists loyal, Danton and Camille Desmoulins were sent to prison , and was released on April 5th after a trial for the program which could have done more harm in the case of Robespierre more than every other action in the time.

The Law of 22 Prairial (10 June) removed the right to self-defense against "opponents of the common people." Prisoners in the provinces would be transported to Paris to stand trial. Between April and July the frequency executed in Paris increased from 5 to 26 per day. The majority of Jacobins mocked at the Cult of the Supreme Being celebration on the 8th of June in a lavish and costly performance which was hosted by Robespierre who was involved in spreading false assertions that he was a second Messiah. A heightened agitation amongst the sans-culottes was caused by the loosening of cost policies as well as the extreme inflation, however the increased military position eased fears that the republic was at risk. Many feared that the demise of Robespierre could threaten their security. Three Members of the Committee of Public Security announced that he was a totalitarian in his presence at the conference held on the 29th of June.

Robespierre was rebuffed by refusing to attend sessions, allowing his opponents to create an anti-Robespierre group. In his speech to the gathering on July 26 the

26th, he claimed that certain people were conspiring to undermine the Republic which should be proven, will likely result in the death penalty. The meeting ended in surprise in the absence of revealing names. In the evening, he gave similar remarks at the Jacobins club, which was met with the roar of praise and tears in the direction of the "terrorists' be punished. It was evident that if his opponents didn't take action, he would. the following morning, Robespierre as well as his wonderful buddies were exiled from the Convention. When he tried to talk, his tone faltered and a delegate yelled, "The blood of Danton is choking him!"

After the Convention's acceptance of his detention the group of supporters sought refuge within the Hotel de Ville, which was protected with National Guard members. The Convention-aligned system took over the hotel later that night and killed Robespierre who was attempting suicide and was seriously injured. On July 28th Robespierre was hanged along with 19 colleagues, which included Saint-Just as well as Georges Couthon as well as 83 people from the Commune. In the aftermath, the Law of 22 Prairial was repealed, and any remaining Girondists were reinstated as deputies as well as Jacobin Club was closed down. Jacobin Club was closed down and prohibited.

The Horror and the ferocity that was used to bring it about were analyzed in various ways. Marxist historian Albert Soboul saw it as necessary to protect the Revolution from internal and external dangers. As per Francois Furet The revolutionaries' intense commitment to ideology and utopian goals demanded the elimination of all dissent. A middle position suggests how violence could be the consequence from a complex series of internal processes that were exacerbated by disputes and conflict, rather than being an inevitable outcome.

After the death of Robespierre, an series of violent killings began to take place within Southern France, targeting implicated Jacobins, Republican authorities, and Protestants. As the

Thermidor triumphantly took in the Commune by killing its leaders, a few of the people who participated of the "Fear" continued to hold the position of power. Paul Barras, later the French Directory site's senior executive as well as Joseph Fouche, the director of the Lyon assassinations and the Secretary of Authorities under the Directory Site, the Consulate as well as the Empire were among the others. Others were deported or tried and took months to complete.

The Treaty of La Jaunaye, reviewed in December 1794 ended the Chouannerie in the western part of France and brought back the liberty of praise as well as the return of priests who did not commit any offenses.

In the month of January 1795, French armies assisted in the efforts of Dutch Patriots in developing the Batavian Republic and defending their northern border. In 1795, the Peace of Basel, checked in April 1795, concluded the conflict with Prussia to the benefit of France in France's favor, and Spain agreed to peace shortly after.

However the Republic was in the midst of an internal conflict. The necessity to prepare troops in Flanders increased food shortages resulting from the poor harvest of 1794 across Northern France, while the winter was the lowest since the year 1709. People were starving in April 1795. The assignment was worth only 8percent of its declared value. In desperate times in the face of this, the Parisian poor retreated. They were distributed quickly and the most significant impact was a fresh round of arrests. Moreover, Jacobin prisoners in Lyon were executed without hearing.

A committee drafted the new constitution, which was approved in a plebiscite on the 23rd of September 1795. It was then ratified on the 27th of September, 1795.
It formulated a bicameral legislature that was developed primarily by Pierre Daunou and Boissy d'Anglas and Boissy d'Anglas,

with the aim of slowed down the legal process and putting an end to the policy turbulences that had previously been the norm under unicameral system. The Council of five hundred was in charge the development of legislation. It was later scrutinized and approved from the Council of Ancients, a group of 250 males who were older than 40 years old. Five Directors were selected to be selected by the Council of Ancients from a list that was submitted by the lower house, and were granted the required five years.

Indirect elections were used to elect deputies. There was a total population of five million voters participating in primary elections for 30,000 voters that is 0.6 per cent of population. It ensured the election of moderate or conservative deputies since they were subject to strict property requirements. In addition, instead of liquidating the old assembly as in 1791-1792 law of two-thirds' stipulated that only 150 new members would be selected every year. The remaining 600

Conventionnels were allowed to keep their seats. This was to ensure stability.

Chapter 4: Revolutionary Wars

The Revolution brought about several battles that continued until the defeat of Napoleon at Waterloo in 1815. It seems unlikely at the beginning, but the 1791 Constitution specifically forbade "war with the intention of the purpose of conquest," and while old tensions among France and Austria came back in the 1780s, the Emperor Joseph was adamantly in support of the reforms. In the 1780s, both Austria along with Russia were fighting the Ottomans as well as in talks with Prussia regarding the possibility of separating Poland. But, most importantly, Britain desired peace, and as the Emperor Leopold stated in the aftermath of his Pillnitz Statement, "there is no way to resolve the issue that is not a part of England."

In 1791, the year that ended in 1791, the members of the Assembly began to think about war as a way to unify the nation and safeguarding the Revolution by removing the any hostile forces within the borders of the nation and expanding its "natural borders."

In the spring of 1792 France made a declaration of war with Austria and issued the first conscription orders which required the soldiers to serve for a period of one year. The conflict had changed Europe's map. Europe and extended into the Americas and in the Middle East, and the Indian Ocean by the time peace was achieved in 1815. that included each major European state as well as that of the United States.

Between 1701 between 1701 and 1801, Europe's population was boosted from 118 to the number of 187 million that, in addition to new commercial strategies enabled belligerents to have massive armies without having to mobilize resources of their country. This was a distinct type of conflict, fought by nations rather than monarchs, with the aim of destabilizing their rivals capacity to endure and causing widespread changes in society. Although all conflicts are political in some way but this particular time frame stands out because of the emphasis on changing boundaries and the establishment of completely modern European states.

On April 17, 1792 French fighters invaded the Austrian Netherlands and suffered several losses before winning at Valmy during the month of September, defeating an Austrian-Prussian force. They took on the Netherlands and parts of the Rhineland, Nice, and Savoy after defeating a second Austrian army at Jemappes on the 6th of November. In awe of this victory, France announced war on the Dutch Republic, Spain, and the U.K. in the month of February 1793. This marked the beginning of with the First Union War. The French were then forced to hand over their conquests once the twelve-month period for employees of 1792 was over. Conscription laws were revised in August.

By May 1794 in the French army had risen to approximately 750,000 to 800,000.. Despite the high rate of defection, this army was sufficient enough to take on the range of internal and external threats in contrast to the Prussian-Austrian unit numbered less than 90,000.

In February 1795, France had conquered its hold on the Austrian Netherlands, created a border along the left bank of the Rhine and reformed to replace the Dutch Republic with a satellite state known as named the Batavian Republic. The French-French alliance fell apart in the wake of these victories. Prussia agreed to a peace treaty in April 1795. This was then Spain shortly thereafter which left Britain as well as Austria as the sole significant countries still fighting. After a series of stumbling blocks within Italy, Austria consented to the Treaty of Campo Formio in October 1797. It was a formal declaration of to the Netherlands in recognition of that it was a part of the Cisalpine Republic.

The fighting continued due to two reasons: the first was that it was because the French Federal government's finances were dependent on indemnities that were imposed on defeated challengers. Second secondly, there was a second reason: the French Federal government's finances were dependent on indemnities imposed to challengers who beat them. Second, the armies were focused on their commanders and the money and prestige that was derived from success were a goal in themselves. Leaders like Hoche, Pichegru, and Carnot were able to exert enormous political influence, and generally set the policy. Campo Formio was accepted by Bonaparte but not Bonaparte, but not the Directory Site, that reacted with aplomb to phrases it considered excessively generous.

However, despite these meetings regardless of these appointments, the Directory site was never able to come up with an effective peace plan because they were afraid of the negative consequences of peace and the disengagement of many young men. They were very happy to let Generals, and the armies they commanded fight so long as they were kept away from Paris and the city of Paris, which was a key factor in Bonaparte's incursion into Egypt. In the wake of these uncompromising and risk-taking actions and actions, it was the 2nd Union War broke out in November 1798.

In spite of the fact the Reign of terror had a significant impact across Europe and beyond, the French population was particularly affected. "There was a specific change in every French group that occurred on the occasion of the Reign of terror, in the spirit of the prevailing terror," Martinican writer Aime Cesaire remarked.

The uprisings of the servant within French groups are best known in connection with their involvement in the Revolution of Saint-Domingue. Saint-Domingue was the most prosperous possession of France in the 1780s, generating more sugar than the rest other British West Indies isles created.

The National Convention approved the removal of slavery in February 1794, a few months after the insurgents of Saint-Domingue were in control of the island. The 1794 decree, however not used, was only for Saint-Domingue, Guadeloupe, and Guyane as well as not implemented to Senegal, Mauritius, Reunion and Martinique which was the final of which was seized from the British and as a result it was left unaffected by French law.

"The most prominent symbol of Fear of"the Reign Of Terror" is still the Guillotine.

The guillotine was developed by a doctor in the period during the Reign of terror as a significantly faster, more efficient and more unique method of execution. It is now a part of popular culture and historical memory.
The left praised it as the avenging of the people such as in the original song La Gullotine Permanente, whereas the right slammed it as a symbol of the horror.

Its function became the most well-known form of domestic entertainment that attracted large crowds.

The suppliers offered programs that had their names and the dates of people that were scheduled to expire in them.

The majority of people gathered every day to compete for the best views of the sporting events. Knitting women (tricoteuses) created a group of regulars who led the crowd.

Kids were frequently brought to the Horror by parents. The number of people attending had decreased dramatically at the close in the Horror.

Even the most grisly of television shows had turned boring, and viewers had become bored.

Chapter 5: The Repercussions of the Revolution

By removing feudalism and setting the direction for the future of generalized individual liberties and rights, the Reign of terror had a significant impact upon European and Western historical.
It had a significant impact on French nationalist sentiment, as well as motivating nationalist movements throughout Europe.
According to historians of the present according to historians of the present, the Revolution led to the idea of a country-state.

The Revolution was a significant influence in French society, resulting in several changes, some which were accepted by the majority of people, but some remain in the discussion.

The power of politics was concentrated at Versailles and was ruled under the reign of

Louis XIV, whose impact was based on his huge personal fortune, his power over the army, and decision-making of priests, provincial rulers as well as lawyers and judges.

The king was made an honorary status in just one year. The nobility was stripped of titles and estates, as was the church was stripped of its abbeys as well as land. The state was able to control those in the church, including judges and magistrates. Meanwhile, the army was cut off and power of the army was held by the ingenuous National Guard.
The expression "Liberty Equality, Equality and Fraternity" as well as "The Statement of the Rights of Man and Person," which Lefebvre declares "the variant of the Revolution in its entirety," were essential to 1789.

The position in the Catholic Church was not the only one of the most controversial issues during the Revolution.

It was an important place in the civilisation in the year 1788. Being French means being an Catholic. In 1799, a large portion of the nation's possessions and organisations were gone and the nation's most powerful authorities had either died or were removed.

Sundays holy days, saints, holy days rituals, prayers and even events were all targeted to be eliminated in addition to other elements of the cultural impact.

In the end, these efforts did not just failed, but angered the faithful. Opposition against these reforms was the key factor of the Vendee rebellion.

Charitable structures were created through the years to help fund hospitals such as poor relief and schools. However, when they were sold and taken they were not replenished, which caused a major disruption for these groups of support.

In the era that of the "Ancien regime" nuns usually provided aid to the health needs of those in rural poverty, acting as nurses, but also as cosmetic surgeons, clinicians and apothecaries. The Revolution ended many of these orders, but did not alter the nursing services that were organized.

Nuns were allowed to return to work in health facilities and on estates for rural people in the years following 1800, as the there was a need. They were allowed by authorities due to their large support and were an intermediary between the elite male doctors and the poor peasants in need of assistance.

Due to its recognition with "counter-revolutionary" groups, the church was a primary target at the time of the Fear, leading to the oppression of priests and the damage of churches and spiritual pictures across France. The residents resisted the state following an attempt to transform to change the Catholic Church completely by adopting an ideology known as the Cult of Reason, with public events replacing religious ones.

The atheist Hebert supported these actions however the deist Robespierre opposed them, slamming the plan down and replacing to replace the Cult of Reason with the Cult of the Supreme Being.

The French Third Republic ended the Concordat of 1801 on December 11th, 1905. The Concordat set out the conditions for cooperation with and the Catholic Church as well as the French State.

The Concordat was an agreement that brought back some of the Church's previous duties, but not its power, its terrain or abbeys. The clergy were essentially public officials under the direction from Paris in place of Rome and Protestants as well as Jews were granted equal rights.

However, debate over the significance of religion in the public sphere as well as related questions like the church-controlled school system continues until the present.

The current debates over the use of Muslim religious symbols in schools, including headdresses, have been related to the war of the Revolutionary War over Catholic rituals and symbols.

Farming, which changed through the Revolution employed two-thirds the French population.
Rural France was later more of a region of small farms independent because large estates that were that were owned by the Church as well as the nobles, and occupied by workers employed to work broke down. Taxes on harvest, like seigneurial and tithes, were abolished, to the satisfaction of farmers.
Primogeniture was abolished for peasants and nobility alike which weakened the patriarch of the family and reducing the number of births because everyone was entitled to a portion of the estate. Cobban asserts that the Revolution ended the nation's existence with an "gentility in landowners."

In the same way that limiting monopolies, benefits and disadvantages, rules taxes and guilds helped pave the way for small-scale business, it developed in cities.
The British embargo, on contrary, successfully prevented trade between the settler and international markets affected towns and supply networks to be affected.
I
In generalsense, generally speaking, Revolution did not have a significant impact to overall French business system. It could have helped to thaw the eyes of small-scale business owners. A huge market was more rare as in other countries with industrialization and the typical business owner had a small mill, store or shop, and had assistance from family members and perhaps a salaried employees.

Experts in economic history debate whether the exodus of over 100,000 people in the Revolution with the vast majority of whom were supporters of the previous practice, had any impact on per capita salaries.

One theory is that the subsequent fragmentation of farms caused a negative impact in the beginning of the 19th century however, the situation changed during the second part of the century, as it helped to develop human capital expenditure.

Others believe that the redistribution of land has had a rapid positive impact on efficiency in farming, which was then slowly diminished throughout the 19th century.

The Revolution ended the approximate monarchy and promised lawful rule within the framework of a constitutional order however, it did not eliminate the possibility of an absolute monarchy.

As emperor Napoleon established a constitutional order (albeit it was a totality of his power) and the returned Bourbons were forced to accept the system.

The monarchists were able to vote in a large following Napoleon III's abdication in

1871, however they were so dispersed that they were unable to agree on who should reign as king and they created the French Third Republic was established with a strong commitment to defending the values of the Revolution.

Vichy France (1940 from 1940 to 1944) was run by conservative Catholics who tried, but were unsuccessful to end the tradition of the Revolution, however they kept the country an independent republic.

Vichy rejected the idea of equality, preferring "Work, Family, and Fatherland" in lieu of the Revolutionary slogans "Liberty and Equality Fraternity." Vichy, the Bourbons, Vichy, or any other person, on the contrary, made no attempt to re-enforce the privileges that were removed from the nobility during 1789.

According to the laws, France developed a civilization of equates for the duration of time.

The Reign of terror has gotten an abundance of attention in the past in the media, as well as from the general public and from chroniclers as well as academics. Viewpoints regarding its significance and significant developments are usually grouped by ideological divides.

It is generally accepted that Revolutionary War research studies initially focused on political concepts and things, but gradually moved to a more social historical perspective that examined the effects of the Revolution on the lives of people.

Conservatives such as Edmund Burke and Friedrich von Gentz claimed that revolutionaries were influenced to defeat the old order by a few conspiratorial individuals, a belief is based on the idea that revolutionaries had no actual concerns.

At the turn of 19th-century, financial specialists as well as political scholars such as Alexis de Tocqueville evaluated the Revolution extensively, concluding that it was the result of a flourishing middle class, conscious of its social responsibility.

Karl Marx was maybe the most famous, because Marx saw the Revolution's class nature as vital in understanding human progress. He claimed that the egalitarian principles they promoted led to the birth of "socialism," an egalitarian and cooperative model of social cohesion that was manifested during The 1870-1871 Paris Commune.

Through much of the twentieth century Marxist historical writers, such as Albert Soboul, highlighted the involvement of peasants as well as urban workers during the Revolution and presented the Revolution as a struggle for class.

The main thrust in this debate was the fact that the Revolution was born out of the growing middle class, aided by the sans-culottes who teamed up to take on the nobility. However, in the 1990s,
Western scientists mostly rejected Marxist studies; the concept of class warfare had gained general disrepute, but the alternative explanations had not gained

widespread acceptance. But it is true that the Revolution is still seen as a crucial moment in and the Early as well as Late Modern periods in Western history, and therefore as one of the most significant historical events.

Within France the Revolution inflicted irreparable damage to the authority of the upper classes and depleted the church's funds however both organisations held firm despite the damages they suffered. Following when the First French Empire broke down in 1815, the French citizens lost a lot of their rights and privileges they enjoyed in the midst of the Revolution however, they recollected the period's participation-based political system. According to one historian: "Countless men and even women gained real experience in politics through reading, discussing and listening to the latest ways to vote in new organizations, and then taking part in marches for their ideal political ideas. The revolution ended up becoming an initiation ritual, and republicanism was an option."

Chapter 6: The GATHERING STORM

"In France, the judiciary along with the nobles, the clergy, and the wealthy provided the initial spark for the revolutionary movement. The masses were on the scene afterward. The people who gave the initial decision have long since regretted (the revolution)]... however it was the people who initiated the revolution. If they had not resisted, and their miscalculated assumptions, the country would be still subjugated to the rule of the state."

~ Maximilien Robespierre, 1793

It was the perfectly stormy day for King France, Louis XVI. His father, the previous King of France, had quit Louis with an enormous amount of debt due to during the Seven Years War in North America that ended badly to the French. In the end, they lost and were forced to surrender all of their North American holdings including the wealthy settlement of Canada. In the following years, Louis XVI had decided to assist Americans. Americans in their fight to gain independence from the British who, even though they was successful, it had forced the French Treasury into additional debt. While the war was won by France's side but it also introduced the idea of a new, constitutional society where everyone was equal on those who lived in France.

Additionally, France was suffering from constant shortages of grain. Bread was the main food source of the typical French citizen. However, an experiment with an open economy in the field of grains, coupled with years of drought had caused the cost and availability of grains to fluctuate dramatically. This caused hunger and constant riots. Without money in the Treasury, Louis did not have the means to purchase grains from other countries to fill the gap.

While it was a disaster but the integrity of his credibility was much more crucial. He was the monarch of France was supposed to ensure that the grain was readily available to all his citizens. The King was considered to be "le most renowned baker du Royaume" -which means "the best baker of the kingdom" So this food shortage meant the King was not performing his job as a primary one. His stature was deteriorating in comparison to his grandfather, the previous King Louis XV who was known as the "Baker King" due to his passion for bread and his excellent management of the grains for the nation.

Louis was left with no other alternative. He was forced to figure out a way to pay off his debt. However, when he tried to approach the aristocracy and Church, all of whom owned large estates however, they paid almost no taxes, they flatly did not accept. Two years later, after looking the issue, he concluded that he needed to call a meeting known as the Estates-General , which hadn't been held in over a hundred years. The Estates-General consisted of three estates The First Estate was composed of clergy, while the second Estate comprised of nobility, and the third Estate consisted of the ordinary citizens.

On the 24th of January 1789, King George III announced the following decree that will convene the Estates-General "We require an assembly of our loyal subjects to help us overcome every obstacle we face with regard to the state of our financial situation. ..."

Around 1200 delegate were to be elected: approximately 300 for clergy 300 for nobles and 600 for commoners. Each tax district chose its delegate. The turnout was very excellent in The Third Estate which not only comprised commoners, but also some nobles and clergy who had made the decision to become part of in the Third Estate.

The Estates-General gathered on May 5th 1789, 1789, they convened in a grand courtyard located not away near Versailles Palace. Versailles Palace. The clergy and nobility were given the best seats while people belonging to the Third Estate were put at the back as per the convention. The members from members of the Third Estate were informed that regardless of their greater amount of delegates, each estate would be entitled to an equal vote , even although they were the Third Estate represented more than 90 percent of the people across the nation.

Then, squabbles began to break out between the various estates over the amount of power each estate should enjoy, and lasted until the middle of June. The Third Estate simply broke off negotiations and declared it as an official National Assembly which had the authority to create laws and govern. Furious, Louis left the hall in which the new National Assembly had been meeting. All members of this National Assembly who had now was joined by clergy members and nobility, gathered on a tennis court enclosed.

On the 20th of June 1789, in a state of rage and spotting that they held the advantage, the delegates took what was later called"the Tennis Court Oath (Serment du Jeu de Paume). The majority of them signed the oath vowing to "not to disperse from each other, and to meet whenever circumstances demand, up until the constitutional monarchy is enacted." Although they were a step forward but the majority believed, at the time, that they would create the constitutional monarchy, as well as that King whom they most loved, would continue to be the King. It would take three years before the complete revolution to take place.

Note that the title of the legislative body was changed numerous times throughout the Revolution but was generally kept the word Assembly in the name. Therefore, in this eBook the term Assembly is used to refer to the legislative body, even though the exact title is often altered each year.

However, the situation was still far from being to be settled. When the King dismissed his most popular finance minister, Necker, and restructured his finance ministry, the supporters who were part of the Third Estate feared the worst. They believed that the troops they were bringing into Paris could be used to close this new Assembly and to restore an elected conservative government. The people of Paris took to the streets to protest.

The morning of July 14th, Third Estate partisans in Paris captured 30,000 guns which were kept in the Hotel des Invalides. They managed to do this with little resistance. But, they weren't in a position to take powder or shots. The evidence they found was being moved in a deliberate manner and kept in the Bastille which was a fortress of the royal family that was thought to be secure and was not able to be accessed.

A crowd of about 1000 people marched towards the Bastille and demanded to receive the gunpowder. For hours The Governor of Bastille was in negotiations with representatives of the crowd. At last, the crowd began to attack and the soldiers opened fire. A hundred people died or were mortally wounded. At this moment the Governor of the Bastille was forced to surrender and gave up. The Governor was then stabbed until he passed out, the head was removed off from his body and put on the pike.

"Wewere able to see two heads of blood on pikes. They were believed to be heads of Marquis de Launay, Governor of the Bastille as well as of Monsieur Flesselles, Prevot des Marchands. It was an eerie and horrifying scene! ... In shock and disgusted by the scene We immediately took refuge off the street."

~ Doctor Edward Rigby

Although there were just the handful of prisoners who were who were held in the Bastille the castle was a long-running hated emblem of royal influence and abuse. Everyone was aware of the Bastille and its reputation as a horrible prison for anyone who dare to question the authority of the monarch. It became the ideal symbol of the end of the "old regime" and the birth of the modern French nation.

The fall of Bastille "Gave an outline and image to the vices which the revolution was able to define itself."

~ Simon Schama

This day is known in the present as Bastille Day, in English and is thought to be as the day to the French Revolution. It is a holiday for the public in France in which it is known as Le Quatorze Juillet meaning July 14th.

After the uprising of the Bastille in the year 1889, after the Bastille was destroyed, the National Assembly, which now is known as to be the National Constituent Assembly, became the official government of France and even negotiated agreements and laws which stabilized the financial condition for a time.

Following the fall of the Bastille the period of what is called"the "Great fear" began. The peasants were told that the aristocracy was hoarding grains burning buildings, burning burning grain fields in order to famine out the rebellious peasants. Rumors circulated across the nation. Peasants , in retaliation, destroyed manor homes, stole grain stored in storage and also armed themselves. The resulting unrest was being among the first significant actions by the National Constituent Assembly. On the 4th of August 1789 the Assembly decided to ban feudalism. This outdated system had gone out of fashion in the majority of European nations by the time however it was a revolution that brought it to bring it back in France.

But the fact is, as one delegate pointed out the Assembly did not think more than just end feudalism. The peasants who lived under one system now were free, yet food had to be produced, transported to the market and then distributed. In reality, there was no plan for the future; the Revolutionaries only wanted to break up the old system and start something different. Thus, in random events, the new system would come to existence, however extreme food shortages would persist and there would be a lot of tensions and the threat of foreign armies seeking to protect the monarchy.

The creation of the National Constituent Assembly and the storming of the Bastille will be the foundation to the Revolution. These were two sides of the same coin. The members in the Assembly were predominantly adherents to the

Enlightenment. It was a system of reasoning, freedom respect, rationality, and respect. They were determined to build an entirely new society constructed with unambiguous laws and a Constitution. However the beheading of an officer who surrendered was a shocking aspect of the war. The mob, then, gleefully showed officers' heads in an iron rod, which indicated that a terrible horror was now unleashed.

3 WOMEN'S MARY'S MARCH ON VERSAILLES

"But people who need help are hungry and they are without food."

"Well then let them eat cakes," the Queen replied.

The story is believed to be the work of Queen Marie Antoinette. However, it is fake and possibly "fake information" because of the rumor mill that was rife at the time.

On the 2nd of October on the 2nd of October, on the 2nd of October, National

Constituent Assembly, composed mostly of members of the Third Estate, officially adopted the words of the infamous Declaration of the Rights of Man and of the Citizen. The document laid broadly, a new understanding of the role of government and citizens. The document was intended to be a part of the constitution that was to be adopted by France. It was also included in later versions, but not in all editions of French constitutions that were subsequently adopted.

It was written mostly in large part by Marquis de Lafayette and Thomas Jefferson who were living in Paris in the year 1789, the Declaration was comparable as well to both the American Declaration of Independence and the American Bill of Rights. In the French Declaration asserted that all men were equal , and that they had the right to freedom of thinking and could act as they wanted so insofar as their actions didn't harm other people. In addition, everyone was to be treated equally according to their incomes.

But, in order to be a legal government document, French government, it needed have to get the approval of King, who was averse to doubts and was not willing to accept the document as it was written. In 1789, in October it was all the ladies of Paris who stood up and made their voices heard. While this particular incident isn't as popular in comparison to that of the Tennis Court Oath or the Storming of the Bastille, it's no less significant.

In the simplest phrases, 5-10 thousands of women walked the eleven mile distance from Paris to the extravagant palace at Versailles which was the royal seat for the past century. The women from the market in Paris marched in the freezing rain of October to speak their displeasures to Louis XVI, the King. Louis XVI. After they had finished, Louis agreed to approve the declaration, and then transfer his court back Paris. They then rode with the King back in his carriage after Versailles towards Paris where he would remain throughout his life. In the process it was obvious that the citizens were in charge, not the King, clergy or aristocrats.

The most famous event of the French Revolution is called the Women's March on Versailles. It is often simply The October March or The March on Versailles.

Women were aware of an important change happening because the new Government Assembly comprised mostly of common citizens, was taking over authority away from the clergy and nobles. The Assembly was in the process of drafting the constitution that would allow the citizens of France the right to vote and greater control in their governance. Since the King was at Versailles and Versailles, the Assembly was also in Versailles and was working on creating a new system of government.

The idea of a march on Versailles was floating around for months, especially following the falling of the Bastille which had inspired the people of Paris. The fall of the Bastille caused an uprising of the peasants in the middle of July. This led to the Assembly to end feudalism and to announce that everyone will be equally taxed in the early part of August.

In August, up to the march the food and grain situation became much more dire. The price of food was skyrocketing, and food became extremely scarce. Finally, the hard-nosed females from the Paris markets had plenty of. On the cold, rainy morning on the 5th of October one woman blasted her drum. Other ladies joined. They were carrying kitchen knives as well as other weapons. They marched towards the Hotel de Ville which was the City Hall of Paris and demanded bread , as well as weapons. Then they ransacked the building. The huge crowd in front of the municipal hall attracted more people, and the crowd had grown by thousands.

This unlikely group of women from the market called poissards, famous for their vulgar and crude language, would alter the historical course. For six hours , they marched through Versailles and many of them even pulling cannons onto carriages.

It is crucial to keep in mind that these women held a deep admiration for the King, and many viewed the procession as bringing their King, who they referred to as "Mr. Good Papa. "Good Papa" back home to Paris.

As the marchers arrived at Versailles the next day, they headed to the place in which the Assembly was taking place. The first time, they were kept outside as a representative from their group sat down with representatives of the Assembly then, the crowd of women, exhausted and wet, rushed into the hall and smashed the members there. The delegates were shocked and were unable to handle the mass of poissards with ease. Then, a lesser-known official, Maximilien Robespierre, addressed the women and assured them that he was aware of their situation and was willing to help.

In this moment, accompanied by the President of the Assembly six women were chosen to go to the King to express their grievances. They visited the palace, and the King was very open to their concerns.

He promised them food right away with the promise of further food to come. After the meeting, a lot of people were happy with the result, however some weren't.

In the evening The King announced that he would take up the Declaration of the Rights of Man without reservations, which was signed in writing in the hope that it would be a relief to those still skeptical.

However, the crowd didn't return to Paris and stayed in Versailles. At dawn, a few women entered to the Palace through an entrance which was not secured. Guards fired at the intruders, and the one who was shot dead. The crowd stormed the palace and slayed the guard. His head was slashed and the women put it on the pike. The chaos continued, another guard was killed, and the Queen had to race for her life on her feet to escape.

After that, things calmed down. Soldiers were able clear the palace of protesting women , and peace was restored. In a dramatic moment of dramatics The Marquis de Lafayette, who was the commander of the National Guard, convinced the King to make a grand appearance on the balcony. Louis did just that , and was greeted by the crowd shouting "Vive the Roi!" "Long live the King!" Encouraged, Louis assured the ladies that he would depart Versailles and relocate to Paris in accordance with the desires "of my faithful and good subjects."

However, the drama wasn't yet over. Then queen Marie Antoinette came on the balcony, and Lafayette was kneeling to her knees and kissed her hands. The crowd of people who were hostile to her were moved, and they chanted "Vive la Reine!" "Long Live the Queen."

And within a couple of years, both the Queen and the King were executed in the Revolution.

The march had one final and important event to perform. Louis as well as his queen, along with members of the National Guard and the Marquis de Lafayette took off in their carriages and made their way back with the crowd towards Paris. While marching, Paris market ladies sang "We will not be hungry and other food items anymore. We've taken back our baker, the wife of the baker and the baker's son." Then, in Paris, Louis took up his new home in the ruined Palace, Tuileries Palace, that was in desperate need of repairs.

According to the legend that according to legend, when Louis reached the Tuileries He asked the servant to deliver him an account that outlined the story of Charles I of England who had lost his throne during the English civil war and was killed around 100 years before.

4 REDESIGNING FRENCH SOCIETIES

"It is absurd and absurdity to say that men who for thousand years been able to berate us, to defraud us, and inflict a sham on us and now will agree in good faith, to be equals with us."

Jean-Paul Marat

It is clear that the Revolutionaries of France were not able to create a practical model for a new society they had many ideas. Particularly, they had a clear idea of what they wanted to eliminate and had a general idea of the kind of society they wanted to make.

Simply put the idea was a government and a system of government based on logic and not traditions as they had been. Yet, at the same they believed that they had to erase the traces of the past to ensure that people embrace the new ways of living and not be resentful of the past.

They had a multi-faceted plan. They wanted to abolish the class society that been ruling France for centuries. Then, they believed that they could build a new society for all citizens that will be free from the burdens of an unjust religion, oppressive taxes, and permit freedom of expression and thought.

The first people they viewed were those who belonged to The First Estate and the Second Estate as well as they were also the Clergy along with the Nobles. These minorities were given the power over the majority of people for centuries and they were finally being punished. was arrived.

The Revolutionaries sought to discredit Christianity in France. This was one of the phrases they employed. Although they wouldn't completely eliminate the Church altogether but they would eliminate the majority of the power of the Church and create a very difficult for the clergy that were still in place. Their goal was that religion would disappear. They even came up with rituals and festivals to replace it.

In a way, the Revolutionaries believed in their own faith, one of the Enlightenment as well as of reason as well as of scientific research. They saw the Catholic Church as a major church of France as one of the causes and a part of an old rigid tradition. It was not just ineffective and ineffective, but also stood against advancement.

The result was that they passed several laws. In 1789, almost immediately they declared the property of the Church national. This was a significant move as The Church had been the biggest landowner in the nation. The new government used the value of these land parcels to fund its currency, which was the assignat. In one go they had snatched away a lot of the power of the Church.

However, they were just beginning to get started. The Assembly was then able to abolish tithes that are the taxes of 10% which the Church imposed on the citizens. The Assembly prohibited monastic vows and dissolved religious order. In addition, they included the right to choose a religion as an integral part in the Declaration of the Rights of Man and this meant it was a sign that Catholic Church could no longer enjoy an exclusive right to worship in France.

In July 1790, the next time they passed what became known as"the Civil Constitution of the Clergy. The document stipulated that bishops and priests were subject to the control from the French government, not the Catholic Pope of Rome. The clergy had to swear their loyalty to France. If they failed to swear to the oath, they could not be priests. After a few years the Pope revoked the swearing. This was not a well-liked policy and was the very primary law during the Revolution that many opposed to, particularly those who were religious in rural areas.

The campaign to eliminate Christianity in France was extremely polarizing. It caused a division with the Pope , who ultimately rejected the whole Revolutionary government as well as its constitution, and its constitution, the Declaration of the Rights of Man. It shattered families. In the end, approximately thirty thousand priests who did not swear to the oath , were exiled , and hundreds were murdered.

In a seemingly insignificant law that was not related, the Assembly formed France into departments numbered in lieu of provincial provinces. Although this arrangement was thought of for some time and was also a great advantage of eliminating the previous structure of provincial churches, and their methods of operation, and also served to weaken the old loyalties.

Then, the church calendar was changed. The Revolutionaries were in love with decimal systems that seemed more rational and sensible more in tune to the Enlightenment. They therefore created a distinctive calendar with ten-day weeks that was able to override Church Holy Days and religious holidays. Also known in"the French Revolutionary Calendar (Calendrier Revolutionnaire Francais) it was in effect for twelve years starting in 1793 until 1805.

In order to satisfy their love of decimals In the interest of decimals, the day was divided by 10 hours. with each hour was divided into 100 minutes, and every minute into 100 seconds. The year was always started at the time of the autumnal equinoxand leap years were shifting around so that it was always on the same date. Each of the newly-named 12 months was comprised of 30 days. And at the close of the year there were five days of celebrations in celebrations of virtue and Talent, Labour Convictions, Honors with an Award , and of course an occasion to celebrate the Revolution in leap years. Year I started on the 22nd of September, 1792.

However, there was more. The Revolutionaries tried to substitute religion for something different, so it was two rival "cults'. The Cult of Reason and the Cult of the Supreme Being. In French the word "cult" doesn't have the negative connotation it has in English. It's simply a form of worship.

The Cult of Reason was an attempt to replace Catholicism by an atheistic system of belief that valued not just reason, but also nature liberty, philosophy, liberty and, of course Revolution itself. Revolution itself. The people who governed it wanted it to be the official religion. It was originally one of the major festivals that was part of the Revolutionary Calendar. The first and sole festival took place in the first day of Brumaire the 20th day of the year II, which fell on November 10 1793. The churches across France were decorated and altars dismantled. In Paris at Notre Dame Cathedral Notre Dame, young girls dressed in Roman dress walked among the crowd, dressed as priestesses of the philosophy. They recited the god of Goddess "Reason" who was seated in the splendor of the robes of a Roman tunic, right next to the altar where it was.

This cult was quickly followed by another cult, that of the Cult of the Supreme Being which was propagated by Maximilien Robespierre , who was the virtual ruler of the country at the time. Robespierre was not a fan of the Catholic Church, however he was not a fan of the idea of atheism. He desired a deistic holiday which emphasized man's connection with God. The first and sole celebration was held on the Republican Calendar month of Prairial the 20th day, year II (June 8th 1794). The festival was a complete success. Robespierre hired the artist Jacques-Louis David to design and plan the event around a man-made mountain which was specifically designed to be used for the purpose.

The Church was not the sole subject during the Revolution. Following in the line were the nobles. In 1789, the Assembly decided to end feudalism. This meant that nobles would no longer be able to demand payment from the serfs . The work the serfs did were now the serfs' property but they would still have to pay for the land. In the years following the Assembly took the decision to tax nobles who were not taxed previously.

As the time approached, and the chaotic and violent atmosphere of the country, a lot of nobles emigrated from France. These nobles were later referred to as Emigres. As this started to occur in massive amounts The Assembly required that the emigrants return, or their home and lands were confiscated. The following year, in 1791, noble titles as well as noble ranks were removed. Then all emigrants were told to return home or risk execution. In 1792, the Assembly demanded that all expat property. They also said that the terms Madame and Monsieur were no longer employed to address a person, but instead, all persons should be addressed as Citoyen , or Citoyenne (French meaning citizens, female or male).

At the close of 1792 at the end of 1792, the Assembly approved unanimously the end of the monarchy. The trial of the constitutional monarchy ended.

Finally, they ratified an act that stated that serfs were not required to pay their previous owners to purchase their property. The serfs had the land for free and free of charge.

In a final note to all this In a final note, the Assembly adopted the system of metric measurement in 1799. This was the very first nation to adopt it. It was the culmination of their love for the decimal system as almost everything that is based upon factors of 10. This was one of their best inventions since this system of measurement is employed to this day by almost every nation in the world apart from the two biggest economies which are that of the US as well as China.

"The French Revolution is the most modernist of all statements. Eliminate everything. Do not build upon the past. There isn't any past."
~ John Corigliano

5 THE SECOND MONARCHY'S END
THE ENTRY OF THE REPUBLIC

"Already there is a deficiency of understanding, a roughness and vulgarity in all the activities of the assembly, and also of their teachers. Their liberties are not open to the public. Their science is preposterous ignorance. Their humanity is brutal as well as brutal."

* Edmund Burke, Reflections on the Revolution in France (1790)

Following the Women's March on Versailles in October 1789, the King was in his palace in Paris called The Tuileries Palace. For the better part of one year, the King and the newly formed Assembly would announce an uneasy peace and try the best they could to coexist with one another. That's at least the expectation of many.

In the beginning of French Revolution, the Assembly took to take the Tennis Court Oath to "not to segregate, and to come back together whenever circumstances call for it up until the Kingdom's Constitution is in place." This pledge to create a constitution was more difficult than they anticipated. The new constitution was intended to be a constitutional monarchy. The King would be able to form Cabinet and nominate ministers. The Assembly could make legislation and approve of the Ministers.

The main issue that was discussed throughout the months involved the question of the King's power to veto. There was no vote, or even an absolute veto which would block a bill from becoming law , or the King could be granted a limited veto, such as those in United States where the legislature can override a veto by the support of two-thirds or the King may be granted a suspensive veto that would prevent legislation from becoming law for a period of years. However, after that it could be passed through the legislative process. Under the Constitution of 1791, as it was referred to the King was granted an indefinite veto.

The historians have debated over whether the delegates believed that the suspensive veto was a viable option or was it the 'poison pill' that it is referred to in contemporary politics. Also, if Louis employed his veto power often and this was the case, it would indicate the constitutional monarchy would not function -- which is precisely the case. If they had instead included a veto with a limit in the constitution the vetoes of Louis could have been easily overridden.

The Constitution of 1791 also changed one of the most important aspects of the monarchy. The King would be referred to by the title of King of the French instead of King of France. Although this may seem like an insignificant distinction however, it was not. This meant that he was the King of the French people. France and not just country of France.

The King was aware of these changes, and everybody believed that he was according to the tradition in politics. He was not averse to the change however, he was resigned to the new method of governance.

In June 1791 Louis was caught doing something extremely reckless that upset the people who had defended him , and eventually result in his fall and even execution. Louis attempted to leave Paris in disguise , and then relocate to the French town along the German border , which was a benefactor to the cause of the royalists. The incident was referred to by the name of Flight to Varennes the situation was not according to plan in the case of the royal refugee.

It was a particularly stupid choice because there were rumors were circulating all over Paris for the past six months about Louis was planning to "escape" from France leaving behind the very people he had supposed to protect.

It could have been comical even if it wasn't so serious. The King was dressed as a valet, and the Queen was dressed as an governess. They were pretending to be the Russian baroness. Instead of leaving with two carriages that were light, like they had originally planned, and which might have been more obvious and faster the group took a larger slow and conspicuous vehicle driven with six horses. They left around midnight, but they stopped to collect fresh horses several times. Just several kilometers from their destination , a postmaster was able to recognize Louis as he appeared on the brand new French paper money, known as the assignat. The couple was detained.

After Louis was taken back to Paris the following day, he was an inmate of the Revolution. The attempt to escape was viewed by many as treacherous. But the Assembly allowed him to escape and, in July, they declared that the King was untouchable and that his authority was reinstated.

However, two days after this it was the time for a massive demonstration in Paris called the Champ de Mars Massacre in which over 50,000 people were present and 30 died in the massacre by National Guard troops commanded by the Marquis de Lafayette.

The Assembly was reluctantly reinstated Louis however in a way they were in a position of no choice. It was the Constitution of 1791 was completed and all that was needed was Louis's approval in order to create it law and for France to be the first monarchy constitutional. In September, Louis was the first to approve the constitution. Then everyone was able to breathe a collective sigh relief, but the calm of this time was only temporary.

Since Louis was granted the benefit of the doubt, many assumed that he would join the Assembly. However, in November, the King rejected an Assembly resolution that all emigrants (French citizens and nobles who had left their country) are required to come back to France "on the risk of dying" as well in the month of December, he rejected the Assembly's resolutions on the punishments for priests who do not swear loyalty to the government of France.

Following these two vetoes lawmakers of the Assembly recognized that the constitutional monarchy was ineffective. If Louis rejected all of their proposals the Assembly would not be capable of governing with their ideas of the future.

In the course of months, unrest bubbled beneath the surface. Foreign powers tried to assist Louis's cause, but their efforts were unsuccessful. In July, a duke who was the commander of an army comprised made up of Prussian as well as Austrian troops issued the Brunswick Manifesto in which he threatened the French government and the French people with retribution in case any harm was done to Louis. The threat to the French people made them of France more angry and also encouraged them to join forces in their opposition to the King. They also heightened their suspicions of Marie-Antoinette whom they believed to be Austrian.

Then, in the month of August 1792, things came to an end. A large crowd engulfed at the Tuileries Palace and was able to take Louis and Marie Antoinette prisoners. This event was so well-known across France that the event was referred to by the name of Insurrection of 10 August 1792 or 10th August in 1792.

In September, the Assembly eliminated the monarchy, and officially declared the republic. At once Louis was not considered royalty anymore or being granted any special privileges. He was merely known by his name Citoyen Louis Capet.

In November, several compromise documents were discovered in an iron cabinet hidden from view (the armoire de fer) within the Tuileries. The documents proved that Louis tried to weaken the Assembly as well as his own Revolution as well as that he was not in the habit of making the monarchy's constitutional system work.

In the month of December 1792 Louis appeared before the Assembly and was charged with the crime of treason. He was found guilty on all charges by a large majority of the delegate. The decision of execution, or detain his body was not a definite one however, at the end of the day the verdict was a sentence of death.

On the 21st of January 1793 Citoyen Louis Capet, the former Louis XVI of the royal House of Bourbon which was established around 1272. He was executed in the Place de la Revolution in the front of a crowd of thousands of revolutionary soldiers. The guillotined man was later laid to rest in the mass grave.

Madame de Stael who witnessed his execution wrote the following:

"This man was unable to summon the determination to keep hold of his strength, and made others be skeptical whenever it was needed it to push his adversaries back; this person whose naturally timid mind could not believe in his own thoughts or even accept the ideas of others, proved himself exceptionally capable of that amazing of goals to endure and be killed."

The Reign of TERROR

"If we accept that a single person [in this case, King Louis XVI] can be sacrificed to ensure the happiness of numerous, then it can be shown that two, three, or more can also be sacrificed to ensure the happiness of many. As time passes we will be able to find the motives to sacrifice the many to ensure the happiness of the majority and will conclude that it was an excellent bargain."

- Jules Michelet, Historian of the French Revolution

Following the time that France became a republic after which those who had pledged to draft a constitution were required to begin from scratch and draft the constitution of the republic instead of an constitutional monarchy. The document was referred to by The French Constitution of 1793 it was a more democratic, liberal and equalitarian document.

But there was a important issue. Constitutional law was never actually implemented. The events took over, and, instead of a fresh model for freedom and brotherhood the Assembly took the constitutional framework in limbo as well as invoked the emergency powers of war. The reason for this was that France was at the beginning of the period that was known as the Revolutionary Wars and felt that it was under attack from the outside as well as inside the country.

The Assembly basically handed over the administration and administration and the administration to the Committee of Public Safety. The Committee utilized Draconian tactics for asserting its authority, and created what was known in The Reign Of Terror.

The Reign Of Terror was what happened following that reign of Louis XVI ended. When the revolutionaries murdered Louis XVI, they killed an ancient person of authority. After Louis died there was no unquestioned authority, and so revolutionaries like Robespierre were quick to fill the gap.

Like two bookends. The death of Louis XVI began the terror and the execution of Robespierre who had commanded the Terror was the final act in the time of massive executions.

In the same way that they not understood their relationship with the American revolution The Revolutionaries didn't understand the two historical precedents they could rely on. The United States, after getting rid of King George I It was evident the fact that

George Washington had the experience and respect needed to lead his new nation and take difficult decisions. In England following the execution of Charles I had been executed, King Charles I had been executed the very powerful and strong chief, Oliver Cromwell, had assumed the reigns. However, up until Napoleon became president there was no such individual in France. Instead the country was in chaos, and fear.

Execution of Louis XVI opened a floodgate however it was one of blood. It is believed that around 17000 people died in Paris as well as another 30,000 in prisons. There were many who died out in the country. It was the Committee of Public Safety in Paris was the actual government that supervised, allowed and even encouraged the execution of people who did not support the Revolution. The committee was empowered by to create the Revolutionary Tribunal in Paris. There was no appeal to the rulings of this tribunal. Additional Revolutionary Tribunals were created across the country and also.

A revolution that was founded on freedom the right to express oneself, respect for everyone and individuality has now led tens of thousands of individuals to be sentenced despite practically no evidence and minimal or even no legal procedure and, in most cases, they were prevented from defending themselves. Their sentence was often based solely on the claims of the prosecutor.

But, it is vital to know that the guillotine was looked at very differently as it is now. Medieval punishments were particularly brutal and the commoners who were executed faced the most brutal punishments. The guillotine was regarded as an instrument for human suffering and also a democratic tool. Death was quick and assured and all people, from nobles to commoners were executed in the same manner.

One man who believed that it was possible to be revered and obeyed, and thus become the authoritative figure of the Revolution is Maximilien Robespierre. Highly intelligent, a great speaker, a passionate advocate for revolutionary ideals, who did not compromise. He was known as "The Incorruptible'. He was the main creator of the French Constitution of 1793 and later, he would be the head from the Committee of Public Safety. It was from this position that he supervised the execution of a number of people.

"Citizens Do you really wish to see a change without an actual revolution?"
~ Maximilien Robespierre

6 THE TERROR CLOSES & the war continues
"When one tries to alter how a revolutionary is going the issue isn't what

to do to cause it to go, but keeping it in check."
* Honore Mirabeau (1790.
Robespierre was adamant of his goals and it is likely that he saw executions as a way cleanse and removal of those who didn't grasp the idea of a revolutionary movement that was so obvious to Robespierre. The peak of his power was on the day Paris held The Cult of the Supreme Being which was a celebration created and arranged in the name of Robespierre himself.
The festival was successful, there was a belief that the executions had finally been done and French society was now able to proceed with their lives. However, the law that was renamed the Law of 22 Prairial (the term used to describe the month of Revolutionary month) permitted a number of executions to occur with virtually no protection for the suspects. As executions increased by more than a third every day, there was enough.

Robespierre was himself arrested and was executed the following day without trial (which was permitted under this new statute). This was the reason why the new law was repealed only a few days after Robespierre died in July 1794.

The period of backlash that followed was referred to as "the Thermidorian Reaction. Thermidor is a term used to describe an event that occurred during Thermidor was a reference to one of the Revolutionary months. The backlash was completely encompassing because not just Robespierre was executed, but twenty-one other people who were in his circle, as well as an additional eighty people belonging to Jacobin Club. Jacobin club that had facilitated some of the earlier executions. In the end, the extreme Jacobin Club itself was ordered to be closed.

In a bizarre rebellion against the rebels, a small group of youngsters began to take part in what was known as "Bals of Victims" also known as "the Dance of the

Guillotined Victims. People related to those who were guillotined began to participate in elaborate funeral dances. It was usually the case that these were those who also received their inheritances restored by the following Revolutionary government, because the administration of the Terror tried to seize the assets of those who were killed. A lot of them wore red ribbons around their necks , in the area where the guillotine was to hit.

Following the death of Robespierre The Thermidorian Reaction or the response to the violence that were a part of the Reign of Terror, spread throughout the nation for longer than one year.

The de-Christianization campaign was somewhat tempered. The authorities relaxed certain restrictions and permitted public worship however they prohibited the ringing of church bells and the display of the cross. But, the disagreements among both the French authorities and Catholic Church were not completely solved up to the point that Napoleon as well as the Catholic Church acceded to sign the Concordat in 1801. It was essentially an agreement between Revolutionaries as well as the Catholic Church.

Additionally, a time of reprisals, also known in the White Terror, occurred across France. These were usually murders in revenge of those who had sparked or facilitated the Terror. Although they were not coordinated, these attacks continued to occur on and off for a good year.

Because that the Constitution of 1793 had never been implemented and was rejected because it was perceived to be the creation of Robespierre yet another constitution was needed to be created. The result was 1795's Constitution of 1795 which was one of the most conservative documents to create an independent republic.

The most significant part of the document was the establishment of The

Directory. It was the executive part of the government, which consisted of five persons. The Directory was responsible for the administration in France until 1799, when Napoleon was able to stage an uprising and take over.

However, with all the political crossing-currents, there was obviously an attempt made to take over the Jacobins Jacobins to regain control they had enjoyed throughout the Terror. Also known as"the" Conspiracy of the Equality it was an attempt to overthrow the government by the form of a coup. A coalition of Jacobin and socialists and socialists, this group demanded the implementation of Robert de la Robespierre's Constitution of 1793. The government was however well-adjusted to the situation. It had snuck into groups of dissidents and detained the bulk of them prior to the coup attempt was able to take place. The majority those who led them were executed following lengthy trial.

While the Revolution was turbulent from beginning but there was a second facet to the chaos. France was involved in conflicts with various European powers starting in 1792 to the time Napoleon assumed power and was regarded as to be the conclusion of the Revolution. There were also numerous protests in opposition to the Revolution in France because of the widespread hunger and Royalist rebels.

In 1791 one of the brothers of Marie Antoinette, Leopold II who was the head of the Holy Roman Empire wrote via an open document dubbed"the" Padua Circular, that the principal powers of Europe unify to attack France and help to restore Louis XVI. This was followed, approximately one month later, with the Declaration of Pillnitz between Leopold and the King of Prussia that urged the European elite to think about fighting in the face of the Revolution.

In 1792, the hot-blooded Revolutionaries were fed up with these threats and declared war against Austria in 1792 as well as on the Holy Roman Empire. In the beginning the Revolutionary troops were disorganized and dispersed when confronted with firing from the enemy. But around this time, as we mentioned earlier the Duke of Brunswick released the Brunswick Manifesto in which he pledged to invade the country and reinstate the power and authority of the French King and imprison any person who was opposed to his. The Manifesto was able to have the same impact on the battlefield that it had done in Paris. The French soldiers were furious by the idea that a foreigner was trying to control how their King would be treated by his own citizens. Therefore, the French Revolutionaries reacted swiftly and were able to regroup with new troops and defeated the invaders.

In 1793, following the death by King Louis XVI, European countries came together in what came to be known in the First Coalition which lasted until

1797. It was comprised comprising Britain, Spain, Naples and the Netherlands as well as Spain, the Netherlands, Naples Holy Roman Empire, Portugal and the Grand-Duke of Tuscany. France introduced a system of conscription in mass to combat the war and remained in the fight to ensure that their soldiers could live off of the terrain.

In 1795, when in 1795, when the Revolutionary Directory government was taking control, a royalist army with strong support from the British as well as French nobles, walked on the streets of Paris. The Revolution contained only 5,000 troops against a total of 30,000 which meant that the prospects were grim. Then a general of his name Napoleon Bonaparte took charge on the condition that he would be granted a full hand. He demanded that forty cannons be brought in immediately from an area outside of Paris and then placed in the key locations and filled with grapeshot. When the royalist army was advancing, the cannons were destroyed. Bonaparte led the battle for throughout the whole time, but his horse was slain from beneath him. In the final battle, he was seen as the hero of the revolution, and was appointed commander of a huge force in Italy. The battle is referred to by the name of 13 Vendemiaire -- the date of the fight is listed on the Revolutionary calendar.

The First Coalition War was followed by the War of the Second Coalition that lasted from 1802 to 1803. The coalition was comprised of Austria, Britain, the Ottoman Empire Russia, Portugal, Naples, Sweden, and a variety of German principalities. Thus, Revolutionary France was in conflict with nearly all European power at one time or at a different time.

Except for the major naval defeat suffered by British British at The Battle of the Nile the French were victorious in most of their wars and expanded their territories they controlled by a significant amount.

In the following year, Napoleon Bonaparte came to Paris and staged a bloodless coup on the 9th of November 1799. He was the first to take over the Directory and closed its legislative body, which was the Council of Five Hundred. Then, he was appointed as First Counsel for the duration of ten years. He then crafted an entirely new constitution, referred to by the name of Constitution of the Year VIII (1799) that gave the First Counsel almost dictatorial power. However, it was one of only a few constitutions from the Revolution that didn't include an explicit Declaration of Rights.

The takeover is regarded as the final act to the French Revolution and the beginning of the Napoleonic period. There was however, in a sense, just one additional game to play.

Napoleon wrote what is now called"the" Napoleonic Code. Although it was not the first lawful code intended for use by the civil population but this was the very first code one that contained several of the ideas of Revolution. Napoleon developed this code due to the fact that the centuries of "old regime" laws and customs were often confusing inconsistency and unclear. The code clarified the rights of people and their responsibilities under the law.

It was also an inspiration for many other nations, and they have all used it to the present. It has been utilized worldwide as an example and is considered among the very few papers that have had a profound impact on the world.

Chapter 7: The background and the French Revolution

In the the 16th century France in the 16th century under Louis XV was involved in a variety of wars throughout Europe and in the Americas. Louis XV was celebrated as the hero of his day, but his economic and political policies led France into a decade of uncertainty under his successor. He was so detested in the years following his death the statue of him was taken down during the French Revolution.

The war of the Seven Years as well as the shortcomings of the king's administration, plunged France into turmoil that damaged the monarchy, making daily living miserable for the commoner. Louis XV has been described in the books of history as a ruler who disappointed his people and delegated the administration in the administration of state over to the ministers. He was a beautiful man who had solid Christian principles, however his failures as a ruler cast a shadow over his legacy as well as the legacy of his son.

Today, many Frenchmen consider the time under Louis XV and Louis XVI as a shambolic and unimportant sequence of mishaps that they would like to forget. Louis XV was also infamous for his love for women and extravagant lifestyle. Maybe his failings could be explained by being the fact that he took over the throne at just five years old. He was surrounded by a myriad of advisors and guardians who made sure that he did not attain the degree of self-reliance and wisdom that is required to be an absolute monarch to succeed. He was, in a strange way, called "Louis the beloved" by his people, but maybe just because of misplaced loyalty or an egocentric attitude.

It was during Louis XV's reign voiced voices that were growing in the Enlightenment class began to gain traction within French society.

Dissidents, authors and scientists, including Voltaire, Diderot and Francois Quensay -- began publishing hard-hitting articles disguised as encyclopedias beneath the King's eye. They questioned the financial policies and decrees issued by the monarch and even challenged the relevance of the monarchy in France's current circumstances.

The widespread spread of Enlightenment ideas among the elite might have provided a platform for radicals to take advantage of the assembly that ultimately brought down the monarchy. Therefore, it is not completely true to say the idea that Louis XV was the one responsible for the beginning of the French Revolution and the eventual beheading of his son.

Prior to his demise, Louis XV made a series of changes to the tax system. These changes were not popular with the nobles but embraced by the people. He ruled that all classes would be taxed in a uniform manner, thus removing the nobles' parliaments. Unfortunately, his death reversed the majority of his efforts to ease the burden of the people while making monarchy accessible to the poor. The taxation policies that were harsh and the financial policies of his heir (which will be covered later in the book) are likely to be significantly different from what Louis XV had in mind.

It wasn't the string of losses in costly battles that raged across Europe or America that sunk the monarchy. Louis XV had trouble reconciling the religious elite and working with various classes and houses of the state. He was plagued by constant religious disputes and criticism from prominent Church members. Louis XV was unprepared to become a ruler and his failures were not enough to save his image , or the image of his monarchy. His insanity and confidence in himself caused the monarchy to be a target of ridicule and an image of failure.

Louis XV was also known for his infidelity as well as his lavish lifestyle. Alongside his ten children who were acknowledged and his inexplicably romantic adventures produced a number of unlegitimate children through five mistresses. Most of them also contributed to the poor decisions that caused adverse effects on the nation. For instance, one of the mistresses Pauline de Mailly-Nesle was a key player in involvement with the succession of Franco Austrian dispute and the disastrous result. Louis XV's former lover, Jeanne-Antoinette Poisson, made the majority of his decisions on politics for him while that they were together.

Louis XV's mistakes in diplomacy caused a series of mistakes by France to manage Central Europe and territories in India and North America as French forces were defeated completely in the hands of British along with their allies. His efforts to overhaul his financial structure and remove the parlements from their power while noble however, were later undone by his son, which led into the French Revolution.

Louis XV left for a hunting trip in the month of April in 1774 when he fell ill. He was afflicted with what was believed to be chickenpox despite efforts made by royal doctors and surgeons to treat his. His heir, Louis XVI, who was a shrewd young man was forced to assume the helm of the power. Louis XV died a hated man, much like his predecessor, but not as much as his son was to be.

"Protect us, Lord, as we are too young to rule." That was the words spoken by the newly-crowned the King Louis XVI, grandson of the notorious Louis XV, the indolent King Louis XV and son of the late Louis Ferdinand, Dauphin of France. It is not clear if they were a reference to the shortcomings by his grandfather, who been in power since the age of five and if he was preparing his people for the massive failures to follow.

The reign of King Louis XVI was plagued by problems from the beginning. He did not just marry an opponent state, but also made a few embarrassing mistakes as a husband during the beginning during his union. He was married to Marie Antoinette of Austria, who he got married at the age of 15. The gorgeous Archduchess from Austria and the Queen of France quickly became one of the most hated woman in the royal family and with good reason. In the beginning she was criticized for not having an heir. However, this was later found to be a flaw that Louis was suffering from. In the following years, she was criticized for her extravagant lifestyle and unfaithfulness to the French people.

Over the course of time The young royals including the king became the target of ridicule as well as a source of humor from certain sections of the society. Even Louis's own family members were not particularly fond of him which was apparent in his wedding celebration.

Queen Marie Antoinette seemed to be in conflict in her relationship with Madame du Barry, one of King Louis's many lovers. It was a fact that King Louis XVI wasn't the favorite child in the family. his parents had favored his older brother, until his death at the tender age 10.

It is vital to keep in mind this is it was King Louis XV who negotiated King Louis XVI's wedding with the Austrians as he was in the midst of his youth. Louis XVI was ridiculed for his inability to conceive his lovely wife, however it was later discovered that he suffered from a rare erectile disorder called phimosis. When he finally accepted to undergo surgery the condition, he was then capable of having four children including two daughters and two sons.

But his initial inability to achieve this led to the fact that Louis XVI grew up a timid and somewhat unsocial character lacking the self-confidence required for a monarch who was in charge of an increasingly hostile kingdom , and confronted by an obnoxious and radical elite of the political class. He was unable to deal with the rising desperation and discord within French society, nor the frequent riots and his acceptance by the monarchy seemed to be in decline in the majority of regions.

The meeting of the Estates General
The French population was suffering from difficult economic times caused by high taxes, unfavorable weather conditions, and corruption. The peasants and the poorest of the population were among the worst to be afflicted, and many were suffering from hunger and starvation for a number of decades under previous administration.
The king Louis XV had tried to modify the tax system during his final years, but one of Louis XVI's initial decisions as a the king was to impose more tax burdens on people who were poor. In a short period of time the king's young age had removed the majority of the tax reforms

of his grandfather and made life very difficult for those in the Third Estate which comprised eighty percent of the French population. It's believed that he would have liked to carry on his predecessor's reforms, but was met with a lot of resistance from the nobility and the government institutions.

One of the very first financial advisors working under the new King was Charles Alexandre de Calonne. His reputation is regarded as having a bad influence that failed to turn the fortunes of the state to a better place while still maintaining negative aspects that the monarchy had. Along with that the monarchy was involved in a loan-taking campaign that significantly drained the coffers of the court.

The taxes that were imposed by King Louis XVI's watch included an universal tax on land (taille) as well as salt tax, tobacco tax value-added tax (vingtieme d'industrie) and capitation tax, and the poll tax. The most unfortunate thing about taxes was the fact that they were targeted at average citizens, while royalty, aristocrats, and nobles were lavish and had plenty of food to consume and indulge in during a time when France was in financial difficulties.

The size was possibly the most outrageous, and consequently the least popular of these taxes. It did not apply to the nobility and was only levied on people who were poor. France was one of the top tax-paying states in Europe during a period when harvests were at a low, and famines were the norm of the hour. It is easy to imagine how much suffering the common people were forced to endure in this time.

The and King Louis XVI and his finance ministers, including Calonne and Etienne Charles de Lomenie Briienne and the well-known Jacques Necker attempts to reform the system of finance, however strong opposition from other sources rendered the majority of their efforts in vain. The inequalities, among others, caused widespread anger, which escalated to a full-blown eruption, but not before the largest royal mistake of the century that was The Estates General meeting of May 5th 1789.

Disappointed by the impasse and the inability of him to implement many of his economic policies The king was convinced that it was possible to get things moving once more by calling a meeting of his Estates General. In the 18th century, France was broken down into 3 "Estates that comprised the Realm": the First Estate, which was formed with the help of the clergy (the Church still held a large influence in the 18th century of France) and The Second Estate, which was formed by the nobility (a class of people with an education and a status in society) as well as the third Estate (the people who constituted the majority of the population who lived in France).

"King" Louis XVI had been having difficulties managing the fiscal deficit of his government by introducing new taxes as well as making new laws by his Parlement of Paris. The King was supported by a range of advisors, referred to by the name of "Notables". Calonne was his controller general for finances, was one of his advisors, as was Gilbert du Motier and the Marquis de Lafayette, also called the "hero of two worlds" because of his active participation in North American wars that had nearly bankrupted the government of Louis XV. Brienne became a part of the Notables after Calonne was exiled and placed as the finance controller. The Notables were working on brainstorming ideas to submit to the King in the form of proposals. It is Lafayette who suggested a gathering with the Estates General to the finance controller as a method of getting around the recalcitrant Parlement. In frustration or lack of inspiration, Brienne forwarded the suggestion to King Louis XVI.

The Estates General, however, was not regarded as a credible institution that could be engaged in any meaningful activity according to the ideals of monarchy. Many considered it outdated, unrelated to the monarchy, and perhaps beneficial as an advisory body. In fact the Estates General had not in session in more than two hundred years. So it came as no surprise that the King Louis XVI was not thrilled over Brienne and Lafayette's plans. King Louis XVI showed his disapproval by dissolving the entire organization of Notables and ensuring that all laws had to pass through Paris's Parlement of Paris.

What ensued was a series of frustrations , as the Parlement was unable to agree with the ideas of the King and pushed him over the edge. At one point, an angry monarch Louis XVI invaded a session dressed in hunting attire and demanded that the Parlement register his edicts that were not well-liked. The tactic could have worked but due to a technicality discovered through the Duc d'Orleans concerning the purpose of the meeting and the legality to sign edicts at that time. The king was defeated, and his hunting party left the Parlement session. However, Louis then retaliated by directing to arrest the Duc d'Orleans along with his conspirators.

This only strengthened the determination that the other members of the Parlement to oppose all decisions taken by the King. It's important to remember that prior French monarchs generally enjoyed a monopoly in having their say with the Parlement However, the emergence of political and revolutionary groups caused a lot of difficulty the way for Louis XVI.

In the face of the impasse with Parlement of Paris, and the Parlement of Paris not having a clear end the king made the decision to eliminate the institution completely to be replaced by different institutions, including the Grand Bailliages and the Plenary Court. There was massive opposition against this decision and a leak into Parlement which was assisted by the press of the government and Jean-Jacques Duval duval d'Epremesnil, a the government to write self-protection legislation. But this didn't hinder the king or his associates from arresting opposition and locking lawmakers out of the premises which they had been operating out of.

The new institutions were not able to take the power in the manner they had planned. The regional parlements in the other regions declined to signify the king's decrees. The conflict between the king's commissioners as well as the parlements led to massive riots. Members of a political group called the Bretons were detained. In the end, the King finally embraced the idea of calling an estates general. Estates General.

In the month of January 1789, convocations were distributed to all provinces in an edict from the royal family that outlined the desire of the king to call members of the Estates General. The note from the king directed faithful subjects to gather and discuss the financial challenges that the nation was facing. The agreement or the reglement was the second part of the royal decree and the subject of debate. The King outlined an old-fashioned method of voting for Estates General where each estate was given a single vote. This meant that the major Third Estate would always be outvoted by the minor noble estates and the clergy. This was, however, not apparent to the people who lived in the middle as well as in spite of other changes that were made in order to help the current system appear more fair and boost the image of the King that was disdained--as well as because they held a substantial number of nobles and priests to their side, they were not actively opposed to the new system of voting.

The day was set on the day of the ceremony, deputies from all estates arrived at the event in official clothes. A royal procession which was led by the queen and the king was also present at the location. The king declared his love for the French people France by saying the fact that he is their most cherished friend. The Finance Minister's speech was centered on the crucial questions of taxation. It seemed like everything was running smoothly until the one estate rule, one-vote rule was announced and was immediately met with a ferocious protests from the furious Third Estate who demanded voting in head. Trysts to placate the commoners proved futile and ultimately, the agenda for the meeting never came to fruition.

They were members who were part of the Third Estate were then locked out of the meeting rooms by the guard of the royals. They were determined to win they decided to break away from their main body to establish an independent National Assembly. They were quickly evicted of the venue as well, and then relocated into an indoor tennis facility nearby. It was at this site when was where the well-known Tennis Court Oath (Serment du Jeu de Paume) was created. In the oath, Third Estate members vowed never to break off and to meet at any time necessary until the adoption of a new constitution. The end to the Estates General, and several clergy and nobles joined the newly formed National Assembly. The king was left with no choice but to enact his laws through the assembly, later changing its name to as the National Constituent Assembly.

Bastille Prison Attack
The monarchy was subdued by the National Assembly, France sank into uncertainty and fear of the possibility of a coup. The poor, who were unable to get enough food, turned to violent riots, looting, and murder as they raged over their situation. When the authorities took action to stop the riots and riots, many people from all walks of

life ended up finding themselves in prison, in debt or both.

The crisis only got worse after Jacques Necker, the charismatic finance minister, was fired. Necker was a popular figure with the revolutionaries because he took the bold decision to make the royal family's spending public. This obviously had not been a great success in boosting his popularity with the monarch. Members in the National Assembly took his dismissal as the start of a self-coup in which the king was expected to get rid of the National Assembly. And the mass of royal troops as well as foreign soldiers within Versailles and Paris certainly made it appear as if Louis was planning either a round-up , or a mass murder of all political dissidents.

Or, from a genuine sense of self-defense, the radicals were out in the streets. In Paris and the property that was taken was sold on the market.

Every single person was exempted or even convents and the crowds began fighting directly with the troops of Louis' German mercenaries. Afraid of being massacred their commanders demanded a retreat, giving an opportunity to Third Estate time to recruit and form the militia it had already created. The royal guard seemed inactive and the mercenaries unable to be trusted, Paris became practically ungovernable.

The militia of the revolution could not resist The Hotel des Invalides, where they seized more than 29,000 guns. They discovered that all the ammunition for these guns had been given to the Bastille to be kept safe.

The Bastille was an fortress as well as a prison and was one of the biggest structures in Paris with its 80-foot walls that ascended over surrounding structures. Many saw it as an emblem of the power that the monarchy had, while others saw it considered it a symbol of oppression. It was also just symbolic. It was in the Bastille that the bulk of the political prisoners were kept. The Bastille was once the home of Francois-Marie Arouet and later Donatien Alphonse Francois, better called Voltaire as well as the Marquis de Sade and the Marquis de Sade, respectively. The Bastille was a mere seven prisoners, guarded by a handful of retired soldiers. Furthermore, cost-cutting measures had significantly reduced its security. For members of the militia it appeared as a target that could be easily snatched, and they decided to take the firearm and (secondarily) let all the prisoners.

They walked through the gates in the early morning of July 14th 1789. They also bolstered their ranks with turncoat soldiers as well as a raucous mass of people. They believed that they could seize the fortress however, they weren't going to fight if it didn't need to, which is why they sent their representatives to convince the commander responsible, Bernard-Rene De Launay to give up his position. The negotiations went on for hours and in the late afternoon, the angry and frustrated crowd was fed up and decided to take over the fortress. They swiftly smashed through buildings adjacent to it, and began an afternoon of violence which left more than a hundred of the dead. But the guardsmen of the royal family stationed at the adjacent Champ de Mars did not take part in the battle and despite the heavy loss, the crowd was able to defeat the Bastille's tiny garrison of former soldiers. They broke down the gates, took charge of the cannons and then stormed the inside courtyard, and took Launay and forced him to join the chaos of the street to the outside.

Infuriated that his refusal to surrender had led to numerous deaths The mob beat and mocked the middle-aged Launay so badly that he shouted "S'il you please, quite! Laisse moi mourrir! ("Please, enough! Don't let me go!") as he spat and kicked one of the people who were dragging him to his destination, the Hotel de Ville. In anger, the crowd swiftly stabbed him to death. Then, they removed his head and hung the head on pikes and paraded it across the streets of Paris. It became a defining symbol during the French Revolution henceforth, especially when a large number of people were executed at the time of the Reign of Terror.

Astonished by the attack on the Bastille and the Bastille, the king Louis XVI buckled under pressure and ordered the departure all his soldiers from Paris. He also announced that he would call back Jacques Necker and move to Paris (from Versailles) on an ongoing basis. The majority of the conservative members of the nobility left the city in search of neighbouring states following those events on the 14th of July 14th 1789. The Bastille was later removed and its site is The July Column (Colonne de Juillet) in memory of the events of that day.

Chapter 8: Declaration of the Rights of Man and of the Citizen

The Declaration of the Rights of Man and of the Citizen was a pivotal moment in French history, and was possibly the greatest accomplishment from the French Enlightenment movement.

The 18th century of France was a highly separated state, with citizens having no rights or freedoms as compared to the nobles. The first step to end the injustice was the abolishment of feudalism. This ended many of the privileges the nobility and clergy enjoyed for long periods of time. Commoners could now hunt, contest for public office and to worship however they wanted, and the clergy were no longer able to take a tax of ten percent from peasants. This triggered a series of changes that would end in Declaration of the Rights of Man and of the Citizen. Archaic judiciary systems like the parlements were eliminated and the tax system was harmonised to all citizens regardless of social class. The foundation was established to allow an National Constituent Assembly to draft new rights for citizens.

The majority of the ideas contained that are contained in the Declaration of the Rights of Man and of the Citizen originate in the Great Charter of the Liberties also known in the Magna Carta, which dates to the 13th century in England. The document includes a variety of Enlightenment ideas that come from thinkers such as Voltaire as well as from The American Revolution. The principle that drives it is "men are born free and remain equal". If this is more than a bit similar to "all men are made equal" in the American Declaration of Independence, it's not a coincidence. Thomas Jefferson, the author of the Declaration and an extremely well-known supporters of freedom for individuals within the United States, also drafted the Declaration of the Rights of Man and of the Citizen along and with

Marquis de Lafayette, a Frenchman who had served during his time in the American Revolution.

Jefferson and Lafayette submitted their proposal for their National Constituent Assembly, and after a brief discussion that led to no major modifications, the Declaration was approved on the 26th of August 1789. It was evident from the start that the Declaration could have profound impacts on classism and governance in France. The authority and importance of the monarchy was diminishing with the influence in the Enlightenment movement. In a telling way, one section subordinated it to law of law, which meant that the monarch was legally bound like his citizens. This document, the Declaration of the Rights of Man and of the Citizen was also a significant stage towards the creation of an entirely new constitution, which was one of the major goals of the revolutionary leaders in the National Constituent Assembly. This document is considered to be the basis of what is now the French Republic as we know it to this day. The exact content of the document is shown below, as they are found in a variety of histories.

Sections from the Declaration of the Rights of Man and of the Citizen

Article 1.

The human race is born equally free and have equal rights. Social differences may be based solely on the common good.

Article 2

The goal of every political associations is to ensure the protection of the fundamental and inviolable rights of the human. These rights include security, property, liberty and the opposition to oppression.

Article 3

The principle of sovereignty is rooted with the country. Any person or entity is not able to be able to exercise any authority that is not directly derived from the national.

Article 4

The freedom of liberty is in the ability to act in a manner that harms no one else. Therefore, the exercising of the rights inherent to everyone is unlimited aside from those that grant others in society similar rights. Limits to these rights are only set by the law.

Article 5

Laws can only restrict acts that are harmful to society. It is impossible to prevent anything that is not prohibited by law. No one is obligated to take any action that is not specifically provided by the law.

Article 6

The law is the expression of the will of the people. Everyone has the right to be a part of the process, either personally or through his representative in the making of its constitution. It should be the same for everyone, regardless of whether it is a safeguard or a punishment. Every citizen, as equal under laws, have the same rights and are entitled to be a part of the highest echelons of society and to all positions in the public sphere and professions depending on their capabilities and without distinction, unless those based on their talents and virtues.

Article 7

There is no right to be charged of, detained, or imprisoned outside of the circumstances and as per the prescribed forms by the law. Anyone who solicits, transmitting the execution of or causing the execution of or executing any order that is arbitrary or order, will be punishable. Any citizen who is who is arrested or summoned in violation of law has to comply without delay, as resisting is an offence.

Article 8

The law will provide those punishments only when they are clearly and logically required, and no person will be punished except that it must be legally sanctioned by virtue of a law approved and promulgated prior to the time of the incident.

Article 9

Since all people are innocent until they be found guilty, and if arrest is to be required, any brutality that is not necessary to the security of the person being held will be severely punished by the law.

Article 10

Nobody should be displeased due to his views or beliefs, even religious ones when their expression is not disruptive to the order of the public created by law.

Article 11

Freedom of expression in thoughts and opinions is considered to be one of the most valuable of human rights. Each citizen is entitled to communicate, write and print freely however, they are accountable for the infringements that violate the freedom of expression as stipulated by the law.

Article 12

The protection of human rights as well as the rights of citizens requires army forces of the public. They are, therefore designed to serve the interests of all, not just to benefit the private interests of the people who they will be assigned.

Article 13

Common contributions are necessary to ensure the sustainability of the public forces as well as for administration expenses. It should be equally distributed across all citizens according to their resources.

Article 14

Everyone has the right to choose in their own person or through their representatives, on the need for the public contribution; to make this without cost, to find out the purposes for which it will be utilized; and to establish the amount, the method of assessment and collecting and the time frame of the tax.

Article 15

Society is entitled to demand from every public servant to submit an accounting of his management.

Article 16

In a society where the law's compliance is not guaranteed and the separation of powers is defined is not governed by a constitution whatsoever.

Article 17

Because property is a sacred and inviolable right, no person can be denied the right to property, except when the lawful necessity of public safety and clearly requiring it, but only if the owner was before and adequately compensated.

While it seemed that they had allowed these freedoms for everyone however, The National Constituent Assembly almost immediately began removing them from the majority of. The people were divided into two categories, specifically "active" in addition to "passive" residents. People who were over the age of 18 who were engaged in some kind of business activity that paid income taxes for the government, were considered active citizens. All others included children, women slaves, servants, and foreigners, were regarded as "passive citizens" and were therefore not protected by the rights in the Declaration of the Rights of Man and of the Citizen. In addition the people who were passive were not permitted to vote or engage in the political process. Their ongoing marginalization proved to be the main cause of tension throughout the revolution, and this can go a long way in explaining the role played by market women during the revolution's final stage (as we will learn in the following chapter).

Despite its flaws, it was a significant step in the right direction. Declaration of the Rights of Man and of the Citizen was a significant event in the revolution. While the National Constituent Assembly was busy making new laws and debating issues regarding the rights and rights of French citizens, the nation was sinking further into financial ruin and the citizens were feeling the strain.

Versailles Palace March

In the fall of 1789 France was in the midst of an array of disputes among the monarchy and National Constituent Assembly. Additionally, decades of mismanagement in the financial sector and poor harvests caused it to be impossible for common Parisians to take care of their families. Bread was scarce and cost so much in that it consumed huge portion of the income. The royalty and nobility were able to eat a lot and were mostly unaware of the miseries of ordinary people.

This dissimilarity was the catalyst for speculation of a sinister scheme to hunger the poor to death by degrading the harvest of wheat and then denying them bread. Particularly, after the successful attack on the Bastille the common people did not want to remain in their homes and famine in the face of these rumors. The most disadvantaged women, those who sold food items in the Paris markets, were particularly worried over the shortage of food, and they began to show their anger through riots and looting.

However, this was not the focus of the King Louis XVI, who had since his coronation, opted to be ruled at Versailles. Palace of Versailles, some dozen miles away from the city. In addition, the National Constituent Assembly was also situated in Versailles. Because Paris was the capital of the country and also the largest city in the country Many people saw this physical separation as an example of the rift between people and their leaders. Of course the queen Marie Antoinette too resided in Versailles. Famous for her extravagant life and her love of parties She was a snobby image among women who called her "Madame Deficit".

There were numerous requests to expel royalty away from the Palace of Versailles, especially from those who were concerned regarding the monarch's hostility to the National Constituent

Assembly and the new constitution they were developing. With the large number of unhappy Parisians and the king's resentment, there was plenty of men to tackle the issue as well as, after the success of the assault on the Bastille and the Bastille, there was no shortage of cannons, muskets or gunpowder. Thus, the fire was there and the spark that ignited it turned out to have been a grand dinner which was held to welcome reinforcements of the guards at the palace. When the news of the banquet came to Paris in the first place, it completely angered the population that was unable to even pay for bread.

On the 5th of October, 1789, a throng of women from the market of Paris chose to follow the cries of the radicals and marched towards the palace. The first thing they did was raid at the Hotel de Ville to steal additional weapons and food. In the following days, under the direction of church bells and drums ladies from Paris left the city to Versailles increasing in number and determination as they moved. The group was joined by group of guardsmen from the national guard (much to the dismay the Guard's commanding officer Marquis de Lafayette, the Guard's commander Marquis de Lafayette) and later, by Versailles residents who embraced the revolutionary ideals.

Like at the Bastille the mob was not able to take over the palace immediately but instead , they sent an advance party to talk about their grievances. The king granted the mob an opportunity to speak and agreed to the majority of their suggestions which included a decision to endorse the Declaration of the Rights of Man and of the Citizen. He also provided some of the food items from the palace's shops and removed the guards who were interfering with the protesters on palace grounds. The evening began to fall, and a few of protesters made their way back to Paris however, a lot were not content and remained in their place.

The next day early the next morning, a group of protesting women who were camped outside the palace made into the palace. After being confronted by guards, they assaulted and killed a few of them, before crying for blood from the queen. A few armed women rushed to Marie Antoinette's room and were shocked to discover that she had escaped via an unmarked passageway into the bedchamber that was heavily fortified of the King.

In the final analysis, Louis and his wife were both able to escape the attack and the palace breached and guardsmen shot dead The king realized that he was forced to choose other than to accept members of the National Constituent Assembly and move to his residence in Paris. The royals were taken into Paris from Paris by National Guard and the mob the day.

This was the start of the end of the reign of King Louis XVI, greatly reducing the power of the monarchy and turning it into mostly ceremonial establishment. The king was a subjugated public servant and a prisoner by all except name (albeit being a prisoner, he was able to enjoy certain perks and privileges of the status of royalty). Since the majority of his former allies either fleeing to the other side or joined rebels Louis's attempts to dismantle the constitution failed, which meant that the young King quickly was stricken with depression and resignation. It was now possible for the members of the National Constituent Assembly to draft the initial French Constitution that established a popular sovereignty.

The adoption by the Civil Constitution of the Clergy
Revolutionaries of radicalism who attacked their monarchy also targeted Roman Catholic Church. France was a completely Christianized state as was the Catholic Church, a key element to the monarchy's oppressive reign. It was the sole owner of the fertile land in France

for centuries, and held a tight grip on the financial and land ownership rights of the rest of us. Some of the land taxes which were considered to be unpopular were actually paid to the Church and tithes became generally required. There was also a rumor of corruption at a high level and extravagant excesses involving clergy.

It is not surprising that the Church has been a source of controversy prior to even the French Revolution. One of the main goals that the Enlightenment movement was to separate the Church from the government. However, there was no possibility of achieving this, as the clergy was a part and integral to the structure of governance and had a huge influence over how policies were carried out. In the wake of the neutralization of nobility and the king however, and prompted by the concern that the clergy -despite having backed an organization called the Third Estate during the formation of the National Assembly, owed its loyalty to Rome instead of France and the Enlightenment movement thought it was the right time to take action. They found allies in radical revolutionaries who believed that the Church was as a hindrance against the changes they wanted to make.

The National Constituent Assembly thus shifted its attention from the creation of the fresh French Constitution to de-Christianizing the state by drafting a separate Civil Constitution of the Clergy which was adopted on the 12th of July 1790. The purpose of this law was to place the Church under subordination to the French government and subordinate to laws that governed the other institutions of France. It also aimed to strip the Church of the approximately 6 percent French territory that it now owned. The document also defined diocesan dioceses, aiming to align them with administrative districts that are civil in nature as well as banned monastic vows, which would end the Clergy's adherence to Rome and set how many bishops in each department; and eliminated the authority to appoint priests from pope. The Constitutional Civil of the Clergy also enacted a variety of other laws with the aim of reducing the power of retrogression that the clergy have as well as reducing the abuse and corruption of the clergy's office.

The Church immediately rejected the changes which is why Pope Pius VI issued a statement in which he essentially rejected The Civil Constitution for the Clergy in totality. He was particularly upset by the restriction of his authority to nominate clergy members that he believed was an attempt to alter the fundamental organization of the church. He personally requested the King Louis XVI to persuade the National Constituent Assembly to relax some of the laws but without success. It was clear that the members of the Assembly were determined to adopt the Constitution regardless of the possibility of an unrest following the papal refusal. The king had no choice other than to give his assent and he did so on the 26th of December 1790. The Constitution of the Clergy was adopted as law.

This allowed the government to auction Church property to replenish funds lost due to the current financial crisis. Additionally, it made it mandatory for clergy members to pledge their allegiance, in no way to the Catholic Church, but in the Civil Constitution of the Clergy. Revolutionaries from the National Constituent Assembly had scored another victory which was making it evident that neither the king nor clergy would stand in the direction of the radical transformations that were taking place now in the structure of the state.

It doesn't mean they didn't attempt. Only seven of the 160 bishops agreed to take the oath to allegiance to France and the Constitutional Laws of the Clergy and many parish priests complied with their instructions. This angered those in the

Jacobin Club and other radicals and they were determined to show no mercy to church or clergy in the coming months and years. A majority of the dissident bishops as well as monks, priests and bishops were slandered, killed or imprisoned. A substantial portion of French churches were demolished or closed as a result of the midst of a harrowing anti-clerical storm.

In no way did all people of members of the Third Estate supported this persecution of the First. Although the people of major cities generally resented the clergy, those in rural towns were loyal to their church. There was a flurry of protests across France and in 1793 the full-blown war began in the region of the coast called Vendee. This war pitted forces who were allies to the monarchy as well as the Church against the Republic. The armies fighting each other fought 12 battles in different cities and towns, and killed the lives of tens of thousands in what could be described as a genocide according to modern standards. One of the horror stories that emerged from The Battle of Nantes involved an instruction given by the commander of the revolution Jean-Baptiste Carrier. After taking the Vendean forces who had taken over Nantes, Carrier instructed them to be secured to boats that had holes in the bottom. They were then let to drown. Men and women were tied in pairs , in what revolutionaries called "the republican union".

Royal Family's flight as well as Capture at Varennes

Adoption of the Civil Constitution of the Clergy was the final nail to be put into the crown's coffin. The King Louis XVI had simply suffered many defeats at rebels within the National Constituent Assembly to have any chance of turning the political landscape around. At a personal level it was his fear that the extremists of Jacobin Club were Jacobin

Club were gunning for his family and young son. Incapable of implementing any of his ideas or control the royal guard, or even secure the safety of the people closest to Louis, Louis sank into despair.

The unfocused king started to delegate the making of decisions to the queen Marie Antoinette and the small group of royalists who were still. They included members of the conservative nobility, as well as church, who were focused on returning back to the old. According to them, the king Louis XVI just needed a area where he could be capable of exercising his power and take decisions without the ire of radical revolutionaries. It's not entirely evident where the notion of a shady escape came from, but it is believed that Marie Antoinette from Austria was the one who conceived of this plan with the aim of fleeing to her home country. It appears that Louis did not feel very enthusiastic about the idea, and was unable to implement the plan for a while before finally giving in to the constant pressure of his queen.

Prior to his departure the French throne, the king wrote an address addressed to the French people, stating the reasons of his departure. Here's an excerpt from the letter, as it appears in Archives parlementaires:

For the French People

For as long as the King hoped to see his peace and order restored to the kingdom through the methods employed by the National Constituent Assembly and by his presence next to the Assembly within the capital of his city of the city, no personal sacrifice was of any importance to the king. If this dream had been fulfilled, he may not contest the loss of his liberties resulting from the refusal by an absolute veto in which his efforts from October 1789 were declared unenforceable and ineffective. However, today, the sole reward for numerous sacrifices is seeing the kingdom demolished, all power ignored and property snatched away and personal safety at risk everywhere, all crimes not punished, and total chaos establishing itself above law and even the semblance of power conferred by the Constitutional amendments does not suffice to fix even one single of the problems plaguing the kingdom The king, having solemnly protested against all actions that emanated from him in his captivity, feels it is his obligation to present before the people of all the French and the world the image of his conduct as well as the actions of the new government that is in place within the kingdom...

The king doesn't believe it is feasible to run a country of the size and significance like France with the method created in the National Constituent Assembly, as they are currently. In accordance with all decrees that are without distinction, it is a decree which he is well aware cannot be rescinded His majesty was driven by the desire to avoid any discussion that experience had taught him to be ineffective at best. What's more, he was afraid that it could be perceived as if he intended to hinder or undermine the work of the National Constituent Assembly that was a success in which the Nation had such a keen interest. He placed his trust in the wise members in the Assembly who understood that it is much easier to destabilize the government than to rebuild one with completely different foundations. When they made announcements about the revisions to decrees they believed it was essential to organize armed forces which are essential to any state as well as the value of inspiring confidencein the current government and its laws that must ensure the security of property and the status of all and allow the return of the citizens who were who were forced to leave because of discontent with a particular areas, or fearing for their lives and possessions within the larger majority.

The more one is aware of the Assembly close to the conclusion of its mission and the more one notices the wise men being discredited and the more inclinations increase each day, which can make the governance of the state difficult or even impossible. It could also cause disdain and distrust. Other regulations have only added the discontent and anger instead of applying balm to heal on the wounds that are bleeding across several regions... Frenchmen Do you know why it was for this reason that you have sent members of your delegation to this National Constituent Assembly? Do you want to see the anarchy and power of the clubs be replaced by the monarchical regime under which the country has prospered for over 14 hundred years? Do you want to see your monarchy surrounded with insults , and stripped of his freedom as his only job is to create your own?

...Frenchmen and most importantly Parisians and all the inhabitants of a city that his ancestors enjoyed to refer to as the city of good of Paris and you must be free of the lies and suggestions of your fake friends. return to the king you love who will be your father, your greatest friend. What pleasure does he not get from forgetting all of his personal afflictions and being reunited to you? Moreover, the Constitution that he will have freely accepted will enable our sacred faith to be honored and our government will be based with a solid foundation and effective in its activities and actions, the property and quality of each citizen no anymore to be in doubt and the laws will cease to be a problem for anyone and finally, liberty to be based on solid and unmovable bases.

The royal family departed their home at the Tuileries Palace of Paris through a forgotten back door in the evening of June 20th 1791. They were disguised as a baroness, traveling in a carriage with two girls, nurses the valet as well as a governess. The count Axel von Fersen and the Baron de Breteuil, who prepared for every eventuality and had advised that the royals would have a greater chance of getting to their destination undetected by traveling in two carriages. But the king was none of that. He instead insisted on having a clearly identifiable horse-drawn carriage. Breteuil along with von Fersen's brilliant strategy was thwarted when the royal family took an enthralling journey through the countryside, the queen and the king frequenting the stops to speak with the locals they encountered. Marie Antoinette even gave gifts to inhabitants of Chaintrix. Their progress was also incredibly slow, because the coach Louis chose to travel through was heavy. It was constantly breaking down, requiring regular repairs. The escape plan failed just after they were spotted close to Sainte-Menehould by a postal worker named Jean-Baptiste Drouet. They were detained when they arrived at the town of Varennes in the northeast. of Varennes.

The news of the attempted escape went viral rapidly as it was clear that the National Constituent Assembly in Paris was informed by the close of the day on the 21st of June. Royal family members were led back to Tuileries Palace by a raucous crowd of people who were disgusted by the fact that the King attempted to flee his own people. The image in which the monarchs are taken back to their homes as fugitives being snatched away was a picture that would be forever imprinted throughout the citizens of France in addition to it was the Flight to Varennes thus obliterated any credibility or significance the monarchy had gained up to the point of this incident. It was the ultimate victory for the revolutionary revolutionaries who sought to dismantle this monarchy to be replaced by a republican civil government.

January 21st 1793
The King is executed

The King Louis XVI and Queen Marie Antoinette were detained in the Tuileries Palace, while members of the National Constituent Assembly continued to debate the constitution. A few people supported the idea of a constitutional monarchy and the radicals were in favor of abolishing the monarchy completely. The final result was that the French Constitution of 1791 reduced the monarch to a ceremonial role, somewhat like the sovereign of United Kingdom today--only much less important and more feared. In addition in the Constitution prohibits the king from launching any war and from reversing any oaths which he was required to swear, however Louis ultimately accepted it--what else could he do? --and was thus reinstated to (very minimal) the throne for a short time.

Paris was at present in a state of total chaos. The Jacobin Club was fighting the Girondins in the National Constituent Assembly and food protests, massacres, in public executions, and riots norm of the day on the streets. In the meantime, Jacques Pierre Brissot, one of the most prominent members of the Girondins and a prominent member of the Girondins, issued an open letter calling for the monarch's removal from the royal throne. This resulted in a riot on the Champ de Mars on the afternoon of July 17 1791. In 1791, the Marquis de Lafayette arrived at the top of the National Guard, and after unsuccessful attempts to control protesters peacefully, instructed his troops to fire. Many people were killed in the riot, along with the Girondins were then banned. They were still an issue for a while however, and Jean-Paul Marat, a journalist who was among their most ardent critics and was forced to pull out of his popular publication and hide.

After the September elections The National Constituent Assembly was succeeded by the National Legislative

Assembly. The new body was more radical and had the Jacobins having control of nearly twenty percentage of its seats. The Jacobins have always been averse to the king, but now they had the power to order the execution of his son. However, they required a reason to justify their actions, and they discovered it in the global situation. Frederick William II of Prussia and Holy Roman Emperor Leopold II threatened to strike France in the event that the Assembly didn't reinstate the monarch, and France had already attacked in the Austrian Netherlands (present-day Belgium). There was also speculation that the Austrian-born queen Marie Anne Antoinette had been sharing French secret state information with her home country to prepare to invade. Based on this theory of conspiracy the Jacobins who were pushed by Maximilien Robespierre and Maximilien Robespierre, took things to their own and occupied the Tuileries Palace in Paris, where the king and queen were kept, on the 10th of August 1792. The Jacobins then detained the royal couple in separate prisons while they waited for trial.

The King's trial Louis XVI was scheduled for the 3rd day of December 1792. The trial was scheduled for the day of his appointment. the king was brought in the chambers at the National Convention (which had succeeded the temporary National Legislative Assembly) to be tried on treason as well as various other charges. They were read out by the secretary of the Convention, Jean-Baptiste Mailhe, and included:

In the process of shutting down Estates General in June of 1789. (The King responded that he was in possession of the legal authority to take this action.)

Instituting the killing of crowd who gathered at the Bastille. (The King replied that he had the authority to execute the order, but he never intended to shed blood.)

Affirming that feudalism must be abolished as well as opposing the Declaration of the Rights of Man and of the Citizen, and indulge in extravagant excess during the banquet held for the troops at Versailles.

Conspired with anti-revolutionaries after swearing allegiance in 1790 in July. (The the king replied that he didn't have any recollection that this had happened.)

Utilizing public funds to help plan his escape.

Planned to escape on the Day of Daggers in February of 1790. (The King claimed that the claim was ridiculous.)

The attempt to escape to Varennes in 1791, in the month of June.

Participating in being a part of the Champ of Mars murder that took place in July 1791. (The the king claimed they did not know anything about the incident.)

Becoming aware of the threats made against France that were issued by his brother-in-law Leopold II and by Frederick William II, but not releasing the information. (The King blamed this at the hands of his ministers.)

Supporting the counter-revolutionary Arles Rebellion. (The King responded that he was urged by ministers of his to support the Arles Rebellion.)

Not acting on the destructive counter-revolutionary uprisings in Nimes, Montauban and Jales.

Sending battalions to oppose people who were protesting against the counter-revolutionaries in Marseilles. (The King blamed the responsibility to blame his cabinet ministers.)

At the end of the day the king was convicted of over thirty accusations (twice in accordance with the convention's normal procedure for trial). For each the king dismissed guilt and blamed his officials. The King's defense team was led by an outstanding lawyer known as Raymond Deseze, who was supported with Francois Denis Tronchet. They argued the King's cause for nearly three hours. Below is a short excerpt that gives details of their testimony:

Louis was crowned King at twenty-one, and at twenty, he presented to the throne the model of the character. He was a king with none of the evil weaknesses, nor corruption of passions. He was not a shrewd politician, but serious. He was the one who was always a friend to the masses. People wanted to abolish the concept of servitude. The first step was to abolish the practice on his own land. People demanded changes regarding the criminal law... and he implemented these changes. People wanted freedom they wanted and he offered liberty to them. The people themselves accompanied him through his sacrifices. But it's on behalf of those people that the current demand is... citizens I am not able to complete... You must must stop myself in front of the History. Consider how it will determine your judgement, and his judgment is judged through generations.

When the lawyers were finished The king himself got to his feet, and made the following emotional speech , which would be the last major public declaration of the most persecuted monarch throughout France's history.
France:
You've heard my argument and I won't reiterate the facts. In speaking to you for the last time I say that my conscience is rubbing me for nothing but my friends have provided the truth. I have never worried about the scrutiny of the public about my conduct, however my heart is broken by the notion that I would like to shed the blood of the masses and particularly that the mishaps of the 10th of August be attributable to me. I am adamant that the many instances that I have committed my actions out of a love for people and the way that I have behaved, appeared to show that I was not afraid to stand up to protect the blood of those who died, and to keep this from happening.

But all those lovely phrases were just an officiality. The royal fate was already set. In January 14 and 1793 the National Convention decided on the verdict. All except 26 deputies who abstained as well as 23 absentees voted guilty. Six93 deputies voted for an unanimous verdict of guilty. In a subsequent sentencing vote militant lawyer as well as the radical Robespierre was the leader of the Convention in deciding to sentence Louis to execution with a Guillotine. The execution was carried out publicly on January 1st 1793. His attempt at an address was mostly unsuccessful , as the sound of his mouth was drowned by the drumming of guards.

Marie Antoinette was tried by the Revolutionary Tribunal on October 14 1793. The tribunal found her guilty of charges that included high treason and conspiracy with the authorities. She was also executed using the guillotine around noon on the 16th of October 1793. Her body was laid to rest at an unknown grave located in a nearby cemetery.

www.ingramcontent.com/pod-product-compliance
Lightning Source LLC
Chambersburg PA
CBHW050403120526
44590CB00015B/1807